Complementary
and Alternative Medicine

BIOMEDICAL ETHICS REVIEWS

Edited by Lois Snyder

Complementary and Alternative Medicine: *Ethics, the Patient, and the Physician • 2007*

BIOMEDICAL ETHICS REVIEWS

COMPLEMENTARY AND ALTERNATIVE MEDICINE

ETHICS, THE PATIENT, AND THE PHYSICIAN

Edited by

Lois Snyder

Philadelphia, PA

HUMANA PRESS ✳ TOTOWA, NEW JERSEY

Cover design by Patricia F. Cleary
Production Editor: Christina Thomas

e-ISBN 1-59745-381-1

Printed in the United States of America. 10 9 8 7 6 5 4 3 2 1

Library of Congress Cataloging-in-Publication Data

Complementary and alternative medicine : ethics, the patient, and the physician / edited by Lois Snyder.
     p. ; cm. -- (Biomedical ethics reviews ; 2007)
   Includes bibliographical references and index.
   ISBN-13: 978-1-58829-584-2
   ISBN-10: 1-58829-584-2 (alk. paper)
   1. Medical ethics. 2. Physicians and patients--Moral and ethical aspects. I. Snyder, Lois, 1961- II. Series.
   [DNLM: 1. Complementary Therapies--ethics. 2. Physician-Patient Relations--ethics. W1 BI615 2007 / WB 890 C73666 2007]
   R724.C662 2007
   174.2--dc22
                                                                      2006018114

To my daughter Hannah

Contents

Preface

With this edition of *Biomedical Ethics Reviews* we commence a somewhat new focus for the series. Building on its solid tradition of exploring and debating pressing bioethical issues of the day, this series will now also examine the real-life implications of these issues for patients and the health care system in which care is delivered. With each topic, attention will be focused not only on the theoretical and policy aspects of ethical dilemmas, but also on the clinical dimensions of these challenges, and effects on the patient–physician relationship.

A fitting early topic for *Biomedical Ethics Reviews* in the 21st century is complementary and alternative medicine (CAM). The National Center for Complementary and Alternative Medicine (NCCAM) defines CAM as "a group of diverse medical and health care systems, practices, and products that are not presently considered to be part of conventional medicine." A telling definition, for what it actually seems to define is what CAM is not. We will probably be coming to terms with CAM and its value in promoting the health of the mind, body, and spirit, its approaches to the causes of illness, and to the restoration of the balance that is health, for some time. Chapters 1 and 2 in *Complementary and Alternative Medicine: Ethics, the Patient, and the Physician* provide a context for thinking about CAM and introduce the history and definitions of CAM.

Another aspect of how we define CAM focuses on questions yet to be resolved through scientific studies about whether such therapies are safe and effective against the illnesses and conditions for which they are used. An editorial in one of medicine's leading journals, *JAMA (1998;280:1618-1619)*, said, "There is no alternative medicine. There is only scientifically proven, evidence-based medicine supported by solid data or unproven medicine, for which scientific evidence is lacking." Yet, as is raised in Chapters 3, 4, and 7 on CAM and the physician's ethical obligations; communicating with and advising patients about CAM; and CAM research, respectively, we do not necessarily have that scientific evidence for many so-called conventional therapies. How to review CAM under the scientific method is further explored in Chapter 7. And, of course, what is considered CAM will continue to be a moving target, as evidence of safety and effectiveness moves CAM therapies into conventional medical practice.

In the meantime, it is estimated that approximately 42% of Americans spent $27 billion out of pocket on CAM therapies in 1997. This, according to a 2005 report of the Institute of Medicine (IOM) of the National Academy of Sciences, Complementary and Alternative Medicine in the United States. The IOM found a huge increase in CAM use over the period 1990 through 1997, with the total number of visits to CAM practitioners rising 47%, to 629 million visits in 1997. That surpasses total visits to primary care physicians for that year at 386 million. Most people do not tell their physicians about their CAM use, with implications for the patient-physician relationship and the ethics obligations of physicians (Chapter 3), advising patients (Chapter 4), patient education (Chapter 5), and liability concerns (Chapter 6).

CAM therapies are extremely popular with baby boomers, who take a very active interest in their health and health care and presumably will do so even more as they age. And as they age, the boomers 65 and older are expected to grow to 20% of Americans (more than 66 million people) by 2030.

NCCAM, on the other hand, is quite young, only established by Congress in 1998. Its mission is to explore complementary and alternative healing practices in the context of rigorous science, train CAM researchers, and disseminate evidence-based information to the public and health care professionals. Its 2004 fiscal year budget for this ambitious agenda was $117,752,000.

So, with big issues and big money at stake, how are patients, physicians, the health care system and policymakers handling the explosion in CAM interest and use? What implications does it have for traditional patient-physician relationships? What are the physician's ethical obligations in this area? These topics and more are examined in *Complementary and Alternative Medicine: Ethics, the Patient, and the Physician*.

Lois Snyder, JD

Editor

Lois Snyder, JD is director of the Center for Ethics and Professionalism at the American College of Physicians, the national professional society of doctors of internal medicine and the subspecialties of internal medicine. She has also been adjunct assistant professor of bioethics and fellow at the University of Pennsylvania Center for Bioethics. She joined the college in 1987 after serving as a health care consultant on medical malpractice, risk management, and bioethics issues for hospitals. Ms. Snyder received her BA in health planning and policy from the University of Pennsylvania and her law degree from the evening division of the Temple University School of Law. She is a frequent writer and speaker on health care policy, bioethical, and medicolegal issues. She has edited a number of books.

Contributors

Richard J. Carroll, MD, SCM, FACC is a practicing cardiologist. He received his undergraduate and medical degrees from the University of Illinois. He is board certified in both internal medicine and cardiovascular disease, having completed both his residency and fellowship at Loyola University, Maywood, IL. He subsequently received his master's degree in health policy and management from the Johns Hopkins School of Hygiene and Public Health, as well as a certificate from the Advanced Training Program in Health Care Delivery Improvement at Intermountain Health Care.

Michael H. Cohen, JD, MBA is an attorney in private practice who publishes the Complementary and Alternative Medicine Law

Blog (www.camlawblog.com). He is an assistant professor of medicine at Harvard Medical School and director of legal programs at the Harvard Medical School Osher Institute and Division for Research and Education in Complementary and Alternative Medical Therapies.

Catherine Leffler, JD is a senior associate in the Center for Ethics and Professionalism at the American College of Physicians where she works in policy development and implementation in the areas of bioethics, medical professionalism, and human rights. She received her law degree, with a concentration in health law, from the Widener University School of Law and her undergraduate degree from the University of Maryland.

Arti Prasad, MD is an associate professor of internal medicine and the founding chief of the Section of Integrative Medicine (SIM) at the University of New Mexico's (UNM) Health Science Center. She grew up in India and has a lifetime of experience with natural and ayurvedic medicine. In November 2003, she completed an associate fellowship at the Program in Integrative Medicine at the University of Arizona, Tucson under the direction of Dr. Andrew Weil. Dr. Prasad is involved in clinical practice, research, teaching, faculty development, and national continuing medical education and community education. In addition to her duties as the chief of SIM, she serves as the director of Integrative Cancer Programs at the UNM Cancer Research and Treatment Center.

Lois Snyder, JD is director of the Center for Ethics and Professionalism at the American College of Physicians, the national professional society of doctors of internal medicine and the subspecialties of internal medicine. She has also been adjunct assistant professor of bioethics and fellow at the University of Pennsylvania Center for Bioethics. She joined the college in 1987 after serving as a health care consultant on medical malpractice, risk management, and bioethics issues for hospitals. Ms. Snyder received her BA in health planning and policy from the University of Pennsylvania and her law degree from the evening division of the Temple University School of Law. She is a frequent writer and speaker on health care policy, bioethical, and medicolegal issues. She has edited a number of books.

Jon Tilburt, MD, MPH received his medical degree from Vanderbilt University and trained in internal medicine at the University of Michigan. From 2002 to 2005 he completed both the Greenwall Fellowship in Ethics and Health Policy as well as a general internal medicine research fellowship at Johns Hopkins (where he was also a trainee in the Johns Hopkins Complementary and Alternative Medicine Center). In the Fall of 2005 he took a position as a staff scientist in the Department of Clinical Bioethics at the National Institutes of Health where he devotes his time to studying social and ethical aspects of complementary and alternative medicine with the support of the National Center for Complementary and Alternative Medicine.

Mariebeth B. Velasquez, BS is a medical student at the University of New Mexico (UNM) School of Medicine. She graduated from the University of Washington with a bachelor's degree in psychology. She first became interested in complementary and alternative medicine while participating on a research team at the Fred Hutchinson Cancer Research Center, which conducted an exercise-intervention study as part of the Breast Cancer Prevention Research Programs, within the Division of Public Health Sciences. She serves on the New Mexico State Advisory Council for Protection and Advocacy Systems for Individuals with Mental Illness, and is an Advocacy Officer (UNM Chapter) of the American Medical Student Association.

1

A Context for Thinking About Complementary and Alternative Medicine and Ethics

Lois Snyder, JD

On treating an earache…

2000 BC	Here—eat this root.
1000 AD	That root is heathen. Here—say this prayer.
1850 AD	That prayer is superstition. Here—drink this potion.
1940 AD	That potion is snake oil. Here—take this pill.
1985 AD	That pill is ineffective. Here—take this antibiotic.
2000 AD	That antibiotic is unnecessary. Here—eat this root.

—A Short History of Medicine (author unknown)

Have we come full circle in the evolution of medicine? The dictionary defines the term *full circle* as "back to one's starting point," so the answer is probably no. Complementary and alternative medicine (CAM) is changing conventional medicine, and conventional medicine is changing CAM practices. Clearly, how-

From: *Biomedical Ethics Reviews: Complementary and Alternative Medicine: Ethics, the Patient, and the Physician*
Edited by: L. Snyder © Humana Press Inc., Totowa, NJ

ever, with the growing popularity of CAM today, patients and the public want something more or something different than conventional medicine can, in many circumstances, provide.

CAM is many things to many people—from acupuncture to dietary supplements to homeopathy to massage; some are ancient practices with rich history, theory, and philosophy behind them, some are more recent. One of the issues with which we grapple in this volume is how to define CAM. The use of chiropractic therapy to treat back pain raises different issues than using chiropractic therapy to treat cancer, and this further complicates matters. Whatever you include in the definition, however, CAM is growing. In general, patients are said to find CAM in keeping with their values and beliefs, its popularity not necessarily related to dissatisfaction with conventional medicine. As such, it seems to be most often used as a complement to conventional medicine. Patients value both approaches *(1)*.

Some patients may find CAM useful when conventional treatment is ineffective; some may value its holistic approach and unique aspects of the patient–practitioner relationship in CAM; some may find it empowering, especially its self-care aspects, such as diet and supplements and efforts at prevention and health promotion. Clearly, the potential for placebo effects in CAM practice has value to patients and needs more study. CAM practitioners have been said to be "more optimistic and positive" than conventional health care providers (who, in fairness, have among other ethical duties a responsibility to honestly deliver bad news), and "healing encounters" with CAM practitioners may enhance this effect *(2)*. *Healing encounter* is not a term one finds associated with today's short physician office visit. But, it may be that conventional medicine is "less optimistic and more realistically accepts the limitations and finitude of the human condition" *(3)*.

Some patients may use CAM as a low-cost alternative to conventional medicine. A recent study found that individuals who delayed or deferred conventional care because of cost were also more likely to have used CAM therapies, leading the authors to conclude CAM use may also reflect the increasing costs of conventional care, problems in access to that care, and a search for lower cost approaches *(4)*. The authors, however, urged caution in the interpretation of their results.

Patient and public interest is high in this area, but so is the skepticism with which conventional medicine has viewed CAM. CAM approaches are just starting to emerge into mainstream medical practice, as is a body of research and effectiveness evidence on CAM therapies *(5)*. A recent editorial by two distinguished physicians suggested that the research agenda for CAM posed many questions but for doctors, "the most compelling question is which treatments work and which do not" *(5)*. Similarly, a recent newspaper article described CAM research under the headline, "What Really Works?" *(6)*.

"What works" viewed from the standpoint of scientific inquiry and what levels of objective evidence support the theory, however, differs from patient determinations of "what works," and needs further exploration. How CAM works, in the context of patient–provider relationships, trust, particular settings, patient expectations, communications, decision making, family and social support, and belief systems may, in fact, be the key factors in the popularity, value, and effectiveness of CAM. A patient who might hear from a physician that there is nothing more that can be done for him or her (equating the end of curative approaches with the end of care), would not likely hear that in the context of CAM care.

In addition, patients and physicians often feel rushed and constrained by time pressures in conventional medicine office visits, despite evidence that actual visit time has not changed. This affects patient and clinician satisfaction with care, quality of care, and can create ethics, communication, and other concerns in the patient–physician relationship. How to "focus on preserving the patient–physician relationship, with an emphasis on fostering trust, maintaining fidelity, demonstrating advocacy, exhibiting respect for the patient as a person, and carrying out the individual and collective ethical obligations of physicians" is a challenge in contemporary medicine *(7)*. It may be that CAM encounters and relationships have offered patients more value and satisfaction in certain dimensions of care.

One author has said of CAM that, "Against the pride of science, it offers humility" *(8)*. He continues that, although CAM practices are diverse, they share a number of characteristics. They are:

- *Holistic:* going beyond biology to see the individual as part of an integrated system interactive with the environment and social factors.
- *Integrative:* healing requires an integration of the spiritual and other forces of life that are out of balance.
- *Naturalistic:* empowerment of natural life processes is key.
- *Relational:* stressing relationships and their role in the care and healing process, including those between the patient and practitioner.
- *Spiritual (8).*

Taken together, these characteristics seem to emphasize a level of trust and interaction with others and the world that may not be seen as frequently in medicine. "Nonetheless, these values are not, for the most part, antagonistic to the values of conventional medicine. They supplement them. They hint not only at the limitations of current healthcare ethics, but also at how current norms may be expanded to embrace a more holistic, integrated model of care" *(8)*.

Use of CAM may also reflect interest in health care approaches apart from the "hierarchical" world of conventional medicine *(9)*, where commentators worry that for all of the emphasis in the Western medical tradition on autonomy and consent, a sense of obedience to physician authority may drive patient actions, not necessarily what is in the patient's best interest. "Physicians want to believe their authority resides in their expert advice, not their social power, and that consent to their inclinations reflects acknowledgment of that expertise" *(9)*. Do they succeed? Should they? Do CAM approaches offer an alternative framework and therapeutic relationships and experiences that do better? For the healthy patient seeking prevention and health promotion? For the vulnerable sick patient whose autonomy may be challenged? For the patient who wants the clinician to make the treatment decision? A recent study found, for example, that although most patients want to be offered choices and want to be asked their opinions about care, 52% wanted their physicians to make clinical decisions on their behalf *(10)*. Other studies have shown that, as is discussed more in later chapters, patients frequently do not raise or discuss their CAM use with their physicians.

CAM use raises a host of ethics issues for patients and physicians, and questions about how the physician and the profession are to fulfill the traditional obligations of beneficence, nonmaleficence, justice, and respect for autonomy. Patients and physicians are not talking much about CAM and when they do, they may be talking different languages. To date, explorations of CAM as measured against the science of medicine have outpaced explorations about CAM, ethics, and the art of medicine. We have a great deal to learn as well if we are to combine the best of both worlds. Unless, it is merely the case as Voltaire reflected, that "The art of medicine consists in amusing the patient while nature cures the disease."

REFERENCES

1. Eisenberg DM, Kessler RC, Van Rompay MI, et al. Perceptions about complementary therapies relative to conventional therapies among adults who use both: results from a national survey. Ann Intern Med 2001;135:344–351.

2. Kaptchuk TJ. The placebo effect in alternative medicine: can the performance of a healing ritual have clinical significance? Ann Intern Med 2002;137:817–825.

3. Kaptchuk TJ, Eisenberg DM. The persuasive appeal of alternative medicine. Ann Intern Med 1998;129:1061–1065.

4. Pagan JA, Pauly MV. Access to conventional medical care and the use of complementary and alternative medicine. Health Affairs 2005;24:255–262.

5. Bondurant S, Sox HC. Mainstream and alternative medicine: converging paths require common standards. Ann Intern Med 2005; 142:149–150.

6. Payne JW. What really works? Forget hearsay. Here's how science sizes up some therapies. Washington Post, July 12, 2005, p. HE01.

7. Braddock CH, Snyder, L. The doctor will see you shortly: the ethical significance of time for the patient–physician relationship. JGIM 2005;20:1057–1062.

8. Guinn DE. An integrative ethics. Park Ridge Center Second Opinion #7. Park Ridge, IL: Park Ridge Center, 2001.

9. Cassell EJ. Consent or obedience? Power and authority in medicine. N Eng J Med 2005;352:328–330.

10. Levinson W, Kao A, Kuby A, Thisted RA. Not all patients want to participate in decision making: A national study of public preferences. JGIM 2005;20:531–535.

2

Complementry and Alternative Medicine

History, Definitions, and What Is It Today?

Richard J. Carroll, MD, SCM, FACC

INTRODUCTION

No topic in the health care arena has been the subject of more heated debate in the last few years, short of access to care and health care costs, than complementary and alternative medicine (CAM). CAM has been the focus of extensive media attention, numerous medical articles, books, periodical reviews, as well as the topic of talk shows and dinner conversations. Many patients are seeking increasingly more information from their physicians and other resources about alternatives to conventional, allopathic medicine.

From: *Biomedical Ethics Reviews: Complementary and Alternative Medicine: Ethics, the Patient, and the Physician*
Edited by: L. Snyder © Humana Press Inc., Totowa, NJ

Health care practitioners are also demonstrating an increased level of interest in CAM, not only to better understand its interaction with conventional medicine, but as an additional resource for both their patients and themselves. Hospitals and health care systems are struggling to develop guidelines for credentialing CAM practitioners, as well as opening avenues to accommodate care practitioners and techniques unique to their current framework of health care. Insurance companies are reevaluating what services to provide their customers, while out of pocket expenditures for CAM continue to rise. Articles in popular publications outline how to add CAM practitioners into traditional medical practices, focusing on issues such as liability, reimbursement, and supervisory responsibilities in order to include services sought by many of their patients *(1)*.

CAM has certainly become a permanent part of the health care culture and landscape as the borders between conventional medicine and CAM begin to blur. The results are numerous clinical, economic, ethical, legal, and social issues associated with not only the increased interest in the use of CAM, but a reevaluation of conventional medicine as well.

This chapter briefly reviews some basic definitions of what has now been labeled *CAM*, some statistics on its use, why and for what type of disease entities patients choose CAM, and why patients are drawn to these approaches; outlines the major types of CAM used in the United States; provides some brief data on the effectiveness (or lack of effectiveness) of CAM; as well as provides some thoughts/insights regarding health care in general and the role both conventional and CAM will surely play.

DEFINITIONS

For the purposes of this chapter, the term *conventional medicine* is used when referring to what most readers would consider contemporary, allopathic medicine. Conventional medicine would include those therapies provided by physicians (MDs or DOs) and allied health professionals such as physical therapists, psychologists, and registered nurses *(2)*. The term *traditional* has sometimes been used, but that term has been avoided because it too often has been confused with traditional, Native American medicine.

Several definitions have been used to differentiate conventional medicine from what has now been most frequently referred to as complementary and alternative medicine. At its methodology conference in 1995, the National Institutes of Health (NIH) Office of Alternative Medicine adopted the definition of *complementary and alternative medicine* as follows:

> a broad domain of healing resources that encompass all health systems, modalities and practices and their accompanying theories and beliefs, other than those intrinsic to the politically dominant health care system of a particular society or culture in a given historical period. CAM includes all such practices and ideas self-defined by their users as preventing or treating illness or promoting health and well-being. Boundaries within CAM and between the CAM domain and the domain of the dominant system are not always sharp or fixed. *(3)*

The National Center for Complementary and Alternative Medicine (NCCAM) defines CAM as a group of diverse medical and health care systems, practices, and products that are not presently considered to be part of conventional medicine *(2)*. Eisenberg et al. simply define CAM as therapies not widely taught in medical schools, not generally used in hospitals, and not typically reimbursed by medical insurance companies *(4)*.

Renner has taken a more systematic if not controversial approach to classifying alternative approaches to medical care. He defines the following five areas:

1. Quackery.
2. Folklore.

3. Unproven or untested.
4. Investigation or research.
5. Proven *(5)*.

This classification system seems to be based more on the level of evidence supporting a particular treatment, rather than on its historical, cultural, or political origin. Although appearing somewhat dated, Renner's classification system is not without truth. Many physicians view aspects of CAM as quackery, without scientific foundation or substance. Some feel definitions such as one by the NCCAM provide an air of legitimacy that many, if not most of these practices have not, and never will, merit.

Although these definitions vary somewhat, the general themes are practices, techniques, and therapies not considered by most as part of mainstream health care. However, even the definitions cited previously are changing, as many medical schools are now teaching more about CAM and patients are utilizing these therapies for many disease entities as much, if not more, than conventional medicine.

Finally, three more terms require clarification: *complementary, alternative*, and *integrative (2)*. Complementary refers to the practice of using a nonconventional approach or therapy along with a conventional treatment, for example chelation therapy for the prevention of heart disease, along with traditional risk-factor modification such as diet, exercise, and lipid-lowering therapy. Alternative refers to the use of a therapy in place of conventional medicine, such as a special diet or herbal therapy instead of standard chemotherapy, surgery, or radiation therapy for cancer treatment. Integrative medicine combines mainstream medical therapies and CAM therapies for which there is some degree of high-quality scientific evidence of safety and effectiveness *(2)*.

STATISTICS

The focus on CAM is anything but recent. Even as interest in the United States is increasing, Kaptchuk and Eisenberg reference reports dating back to the 1920s in which a leading Philadel-phia physician published the results of a survey in which 34% of his patients had, prior to their first office visit, been under the care of what were considered cults. Kaptchuk and Eisenberg also referenced, from approximately the same time period, an Illinois Medical Society Survey of 6000 people in Chicago that found 87% had "dabbled" in cult medicine *(6)*.

One of the more definitive papers on the use of CAM com-pared trends in the United States from 1990 to 1997 *(7)*. Use of CAM increased from 33.8% in 1990 to 42.1% in 1997, with Americans spending somewhere between $36 and $47 billion on CAM therapies in 1997 alone. Approximately 58% of all of those costs were paid entirely out of pocket. The largest increases were in the use of herbal medicines, massage therapy, mega-vitamins, self-help groups, energy healing, and homeopathy. Patients used CAM most frequently for chronic conditions such as back pain, depression, anxiety, and headaches, with 4 out of 10 Americans having used CAM for treatment of these chronic conditions. By 1997, Americans made an estimated 629 million visits to CAM practitioners, up from 427 million in 1990, a 47.3% increase in total visits over that 7-year period. Approximately $27 billion was spent out of pocket, an amount comparable to out-of-pocket expenses paid for all physician services over the same time. The 629 million visits to CAM practitioners far outweigh the 388 million made to primary care physicians during that same time period *(7)*.

These trends cross all age groups. CAM had been used by 30% of the pre-baby boomer cohort, 50% of the baby boomer cohort, and 70% of the post-baby boomer cohort, reflective of trends that began more than 50 years ago, and suggest a continu-ing demand for CAM services *(8)*. A more recent report, perhaps one of the most extensive reviews on CAM, came from the US Department of Health and Human Services, which surveyed 31,044 patients, finding that 75% of those surveyed had used CAM when prayer specifically for health issues was included in the definition. Of these patients, 62% had used CAM within the previous 6 months. Approximately 19% used natural products such as herbs, glucosamine, and the like, and the most common medical conditions treated were back pain or problems, head or chest colds, neck pain or problems, joint pain or stiffness, and anxiety or depression. This was not unexpected, given that 25 to 33% of all adults suffer from these conditions at one time or another and because these conditions are typically resistant to conventional treatments. Most surveyed patients used CAM because they believed it could help when combined with conventional medicine. Half used CAM initially out of their own interest, and 26% used it because their physician suggested they try an alternative approach to their problem.

With prayer as part of the definition of CAM (often not included in other surveys), more than 62% of adults used some form of CAM in 2002. Excluding prayer, overall CAM estimates dropped to approx 36%—consistent with other studies. Interestingly, only approx 12% of these patients sought care from a licensed or certified practitioner, suggesting a large number of patients are self-medicating or self-treating with the corresponding risks of unmonitored adverse events, negative consequences, or potential substance interactions. An estimated 50 million adults took herbal preparations or high-dose vitamins along with their prescription medications, but only 38 to 39% of those patients disclosed to their physicians that they used CAM therapies. Also, consistent with other studies, 54.9% of patients used CAM along with conventional medicine (9).

Rao et al. looked specifically at rheumatological practices to better understand the use of CAM in chronic disease states, an area of high prevalence in other surveys. Nearly two-thirds of the patients sampled had used CAM, which was remarkable as their definition of CAM *excluded* biofeedback, exercise, meditation, or prayer. About 56% currently used CAM, 90% used CAM regularly, with 24% using three or more types of CAM. As suspected,

50% used CAM because they felt that their prescription medications were ineffective. The most commonly used approaches were chiropractic (73%) and spiritual healers (75%). Half of the patients in this survey also used mega-dose vitamins or herbal preparations *(10)*.

Eisenberg et al. surveyed 831 patients who saw both a CAM practitioner and a conventional medicine practitioner, with 79% seeing the combination as superior *(11)*. Nearly 75% typically saw their conventional medicine physician prior to the CAM practitioner. Respondents felt CAM was better for chronic conditions such as headaches, neck, and back problems, but conventional medicine was felt to be superior for diseases such as hypertension. The authors concluded that national data do not support the perception that patients use CAM because of a dissatisfaction with conventional medicine. Instead it appears that patients prefer a more integrative approach. They revealed to their physicians their use of CAM only about 28 to 47% of the time, mainly because they did not feel it was important for the doctors to know or because their physicians never asked them about it.

From the numerous surveys, interviews, and studies on the use of CAM, several themes emerge. Prayer, when defined as a CAM therapy, is used by a large number of patients. Most patients use CAM with, rather than instead of, conventional medicine. Most patients use CAM regularly, rather than as an isolated encounter, and do so for those chronic conditions conventional medicine has been less than successful at treating, such as musculoskeletal pain or dysfunction, headaches, chronic or recurring pain, anxiety and depression, or for potentially terminal conditions such as cancer or HIV. CAM is used by all age groups, and is typically used by the more educated, those willing to pay out of pocket, and those willing to tell their physicians when asked.

What is most interesting, as seen later in this chapter, is that despite the increased use of CAM over time and among a wide range of patients for numerous conditions, little data to date supports its overall efficacy. What these studies challenge is the concept that one size fits all when it comes to the type of health care Americans use, seek out, and are willing to pay for, even if directly out of pocket.

WHY PEOPLE USE CAM

Patients use CAM for a myriad of reasons, including health promotion and disease prevention, curiosity, the preference to self-treat, cultural traditions, a perception that CAM is more patient-focused and less disease-specific than conventional medicine, because of a suggestion or testimonial from a friend, media claims, a distrust or lack of results from conventional medicine, or the belief that CAM systems have stood the test of time. With the advent of the Internet and more market-savvy consumers, many patients are looking beyond conventional medicine for their health care and health promotion. These inquiries span beyond a mere curiosity in CAM or a dissatisfaction with conventional medicine, but are founded in a quest for a more patient-centered, holistic, "natural" approach to health and well-being. Even with what may be perceived as a lack of clear outcomes data, "for many patients the lure of unproven, over-the-counter [OTC] remedies has been irresistible" *(12)*. Despite its goals of rigor and foundation on solid, scientific principles, conventional medicine must recognize that it does not meet the needs of a large percentage of patients. With so many patients asking about or using CAM, either alone or in concert with conventional medicine, it is important to understand its appeal and what it appears to be providing that conventional medicine does not.

Eisenberg has delineated the following five main reasons patients seek and use CAM:

1. For health promotion and disease prevention.
2. Conventional therapies have been exhausted.

3. Conventional therapies are of indeterminate effectiveness or are commonly associated with side effects or significant risks.
4. No conventional therapy is known to relieve the patient's condition.
5. The conventional approach is perceived to be emotionally or spiritually without benefit *(13)*.

The focus of most contemporary medicine has been more on disease detection, diagnosis, and treatment, and only very recently on health promotion and disease prevention. Many insurance companies still do not reimburse for routine health maintenance. On January 1, 2005, Medicare began paying for a routine physical, but only for new enrollees and then only within the first 6 months of enrollment. Patients perceive a lack of interest in health promotion from conventional medicine and look to alternative approaches. One-third of patients who use CAM do so specifically for health promotion and disease prevention *(4)*, although the perception that CAM promotes prevention is interesting in that preventive diagnostic screening, *per se*, is not a typical approach used by CAM practitioners.

However, health promotion is an important component of CAM. Millions of dollars are spent on OTC vitamin and herbal preparations that are taken daily, specifically for health promotion and to prevent diseases such as cancer or heart disease. A key aspect of CAM is the perception that these healh promotion therapies are natural and hence without side effects or toxic properties. Patients perceive conventional medicine, on the other hand, as having either serious side effects or risks not worth taking, viewing it as unnatural or invasive. CAM practitioners claim that as conventional medicine and pharmacology attempt to purify substances, they remove the essence of the compound that nature has provided. Herbs, for example, are seen as complete substances, with balanced healing powers: when kept intact, side effects are minimized.

Another fundamental of CAM that appeals to its users is the concept that the root cause of disease lies within the patient, as an imbalance within the system, rather than as an external, acquired disease entity. Inherent in this concept is the belief that a rebalance, a reconnection with the natural order, will cure or prevent disease, thus patients can cure themselves. CAM practitioners, therefore, are viewed as facilitators of healing, helping patients tap into their inner, self-healing abilities. Various techniques such as acupuncture, chiropractic therapy, massage, herbal preparations, and vitamins are used to either unlock this inherent healing power of nature or to unblock channels that obstruct the flow of vital, natural life forces. This belief appeals to many CAM users as they themselves become responsible for the success or failure of therapy, providing patients more of an ability to participate actively in the healing process; the idea that they can help themselves and avoid the often intrusive approaches of conventional medicine. The concept that "nature knows best how to heal," is much more prevalent in CAM than in conventional medicine. "Alternative medicine is widely perceived as the kinder, gentler, safer system of care" *(14)*.

A natural approach is also perceived as superior. CAM, viewed as a more natural approach than conventional medicine, is therefore perceived to be superior when juxtaposed with conventional medicine; pure vs toxic, organic vs synthetic, low-tech vs high-tech, coarse vs processed *(12)*. However, we know that mercury and arsenic, for example, are "natural," but highly toxic.

A spiritual perspective is much more prevalent in CAM and forms the basis of many therapies, a concept largely foreign to conventional medicine. Ayurveda, Traditional Chinese Medicine (TCM), and acupuncture all have their basis in Eastern philosophy and religion. However, these beliefs are not limited to Eastern religions. As evidenced by national data, many patients utilize prayer as a healing technique. The involvement of a higher, spiritual healing presence is a hallmark of many cultural belief systems. These beliefs are perhaps one of the reasons that a lack of a mechanistic understanding of some complementary therapies (e.g., homeopathy) does not dissuade users. They believe there is an effect beyond what one can measure or perceive.

Patient autonomy is also a powerful component of CAM—a desire to enhance one's own health, without the need for outside interventions. CAM focuses more on the patient and less on the therapy, giving patients the perception that they are more in control of their own health and that they can help themselves. There is something inherently appealing about the idea that the more effort one puts forth, the more successful one will be. It is not surprising then that CAM is used frequently for diseases such as cancer or AIDS, where loss of control is high and faith in conventional medicine is low, and where conventional medicine has been less than successful. This also explains the frequent use of CAM in chronic disease states or chronic pain syndromes.

CAM practitioners are viewed not only as the advocates and instruments of nature, but as being able to restore the patient to a state of natural harmony. In this model, the patient is the focus, not the disease. Conventional medicine is widely criticized for lacking patient focus—"the gallbladder in room 333" rings all too frequently through hospital corridors. Through CAM, patients seek more health communication, health information, therapeutic touch, and a more holistic, less time-constricted patient-focused approach.

Although a diverse collection of therapies and treatments, CAM attempts to maximize the body's inherent healing abilities, to treat the whole person by addressing his or her physical, mental, and spiritual needs rather than focusing on a specific pathogenic process as emphasized in conventional medicine *(15)*. Some of these holistic approaches hypothesize an influence, or an effect, on levels of the physiology or energy fields that conventional medicine either does not acknowledge or cannot access. Acupuncture, Reiki, meditation, and prayer unblock or unfold an inner healing potential, individualized, patient-centered, and resulting in health promotion and disease prevention. Patients also see many of these types of CAM as having stood the test of time, such as TCM or Ayurveda.

Despite what might seem to be fundamental differences in the philosophy and basis for many CAM therapies, most patients still use CAM in conjunction with conventional medicine, rather than in place of it. This integrative approach would suggest patients perceive both methods somehow "complement" and add value to each other. Obviously, both systems seem to help patients move closer to their goals. Trying to better understand what CAM provides will help practitioners of both schools of medicine better serve the needs of all their patients.

CLASSIFICATION OF CAM PRACTICES

Several taxonomies have been suggested to classify types of CAM. Whatever scheme one chooses, it must be flexible, as what is considered to be CAM continually changes, is culturally determined, and is dependent on the politically dominant health care system at that time. TCM and Ayurveda are considered alternative practices in the United States, but as mainstream medicine in China and India, respectively.

One suggested approach to classification would differentiate practitioner-based systems, such as chiropractic and acupuncture, from systems such as herbal therapies or mind–body techniques, which patients can engage in on their own. Another might organize by their historical roots, or perhaps by underlying philosophy. Although many systems of CAM have differing underlying principles and philosophies, they are by no means mutually exclusive. The NCCAM has proposed a system that broadly classifies CAM into five main categories or domains:

1. Alternative medical systems.
2. Mind–body interventions.
3. Biologically based therapies.

4. Manipulative and body-based methods.
5. Energy therapies *(2)*.

Alternative Medical Systems

Alternative/whole medical systems are those that have developed, and are built on, a complete system of therapies and practices. These systems can be further categorized as those developed in non-Western cultures (TCM and Ayurveda) and those developed in Western cultures (homeopathy and napropathy). These systems often developed either in isolation from, or earlier than conventional medicine (as some are thousands of years old), and evolved independently or in parallel to conventional medicine.

Several cultures have developed their own unique systems of medicine such as in Africa, Tibet, Central and South America, and Native American medicine. These are practiced less often in the United States than the systems discussed here.

Non-Western Systems

The two non-Western systems used most frequently in the United States are TCM and Ayurveda.

TRADITIONAL CHINESE MEDICINE

TCM originated in mainland China more than 2000 years ago, although since then other countries such as Japan, Korea, and Vietnam have developed their own variations and adaptations. Written documentation of TCM has been discovered as far back as 200 BC.

The philosophical foundation of TCM is interesting and quite different from conventional medicine. In TCM, there is a fine balance between the two opposing but interrelated and inseparable forces of nature, Yin and Yang. Yin has been described as those aspects of cold, slow, passive, dark, and female, whereas Yang is hot, excited, active, light, and male. Health is maintained by achieving and then maintaining the balance between these opposing forces. Disease is the result of imbalance, and imbalance results from a blockage of vital energy (qi) that flows throughout the body along well-defined channels called meridians.

There are 12 main meridians within the body. These anatomic channels and their tributaries are naked to the eye, but are well delineated on extensive anatomic charts and models used to guide therapies such as acupuncture and acupressure. Each meridian also corresponds to an internal organ and is under the influence of one of the five basic elements of the nature (water, fire, earth, metal, and wood). Diagnosis and treatment regimens in TCM are extremely individualized. Diagnostic methods or questions might seem unusual to a conventional physician as they are designed to determine where imbalances or blockages might exist, in order to develop a strategy to rebalance the system. Problems in the gastrointestinal/digestive system, for example, might be diagnosed as an imbalance of fire. The various techniques employed would then aim to unblock or facilitate the flow of qi in order to offset the imbalance of fire and water, or of hot and cold, to balance these opposing forces, the Yin and Yang, in order to restore or maintain health.

The various TCM techniques such as acupuncture, herbal preparations, and massage are employed to restore this balance through the unencumbered flow of qi. The main modalities of TCM are acupuncture and moxibustion, the use of natural products such as herbs, massage (Tuina), and manipulation (acupressure). These modalities are often used in combination with each other, along with diet and exercise programs.

Acupuncture

Acupuncture was virtually unknown in the West until the 1970s when President Richard Nixon visited China and journalists witnessed major surgeries being performed with acupuncture as the only anesthesia. Acupuncture, one of the most frequently used and most recognized aspects of TCM, has now been used as a therapeutic practice by well over 2.1 million adults in the United States *(9)*. Acupuncture, however, is much more than just a pain blocker. It is one of the fundamental methods of health care in all of Asia. This technique, which originated in China more than 2000 years ago, is typically associated with TCM, although variations are practiced in both Korea and Japan. Extensive writings and diagrams exist describing the techniques of acupuncture. Detailed anatomical maps exist delineating the specific points/ locations to be used to treat various disease states or affect various organs. Although popularized since the 1970s, Franklin Bache, MD—grandson of Benjamin Franklin—and Sir William Osler wrote about the benefits of acupuncture.

The theory behind acupuncture reflects back to the fundamental principles of Yin and Yang in TCM. The imbalance of these states results in disease; acupuncture is performed to rebalance the system, to cure disease, and to reestablish harmony. Fine, thin, solid, metallic needles, much smaller than the type of hollow needles used in conventional medicine, are typically first placed in a small tube then gently tapped into the skin by the acupuncturist along the defined meridian lines. The needles then stimulate the acupuncture points along these meridians (channels) to release any blockages that might exist, in order to allow the flow of qi (vital energy) and restore the body to its natural, balanced state. These needles are usually left in placed for approx 30 minutes per session and anywhere from 5 to 30 needles may be used. The needles may be stimulated by lightly twisting them, by electrical stimulation, or further enhanced by a process called moxibustion during which a smoldering herb, Artemisia, is added to the acupuncture site. Often, several sessions are required to achieve the desired results.

This concept of unblocking the natural flow of qi (vital energy) is one of the fundamental principles of TCM. Conventional medicine might explain the benefits of acupuncture differently. Studies have shown acupuncture releases endogenous opioids, endorphins, and enkephalins, stimulates the immune system, recruits white blood cells and other substances to the sight of injury. Research has shown the activation of endogenous opioids and through other mechanisms, acupuncture may stimulate gene expression of neuropeptides *(16)*. Magnetic resonance imaging (MRI) studies have also demonstrated quantifiable effects on the brain.

In 1976, California became the first state to license acupuncturists and now more than 40 states have similar laws, with more than 11,000 acupuncturists in the United States alone. Despite the prevalence of the technique, high-quality, reproducible studies on the benefits of acupuncture are lacking. Controlled experiments are difficult to administer—blinding the patient to the use or non-use of acupuncture needles has its obvious limitations. Sham acupuncture procedures have been employed, but in a limited fashion. However, studies have shown acupuncture to be beneficial in reducing the emesis that develops after surgery or chemotherapy, for the nausea and vomiting associated with pregnancy, and for dental pain. Studies are equivocal for chronic pain, back pain, and headache *(16)*.

A study recently published in the *Annals of Internal Medicine* has begun to change the landscape of acupuncture research. Funded by the NCCAM and the National Institute of Arthritis and Musculoskeletal Disease, researchers found acupuncture to be valuable in pain relief and functional improvement for patients with osteoarthritis of the knee *(17)*. This was an extremely significant study given rigorous, scientific principles were applied to study acupuncture as compared to both a sham acupuncture procedure and a control group. The study showed significant benefits of acupuncture when used with conventional treatments such as cyclooxygenase-2 inhibitors, nonsteroidal anti-inflammatory drugs, and opioid pain relievers. This study, the largest randomized, controlled clinical trial of acupuncture ever conducted, will serve as a model for future research. As seen later in this chapter, there are now numerous, ongoing well-designed trials to study various aspects of CAM.

Herbal Medicine

Although a component of many different health care systems, the use of herbs plays a major role in TCM. In addition to their extensive use in TCM, herbs are one of the most commonly used forms of CAM in the United States. The Chinese Materia Medica, the standard reference on the medicinal substances used in TCM, contains information on thousands of herbs and their uses. Herbs are used in TCM to bring about changes in physiology, but also are used to influence the conscious and subconscious mind. Herbs are prescribed regularly to balance Yin and Yang, to produce harmony within the body.

Dispensed according to imbalances diagnosed in the system, an herb with Yin qualities might be given to balance a Yin deficiency. This concept is not unfamiliar to conventional medicine. It has parallels in the functioning of the endocrine system, a natural system designed to establish and maintain homeostasis. An herbalist will prescribe herbs based on environmental influences such as the change in seasons, or according to dietary needs. The indications for the use of herbs are quite specific, and herbs are often used in their whole form. Modern pharmacology often strives to isolate and administer the active ingredients of a substance such as herbs. In TCM the entire, unprocessed substance is most often used, with the belief that different parts of the herb interact with each other, actually enhancing the "active" ingredient in the herb while at the same time neutralizing potential side effects by keeping the substance intact.

Many specific factors can influence the beneficial effects and potency of herbs, such as the type of soil in which they were grown, geographic location, storage techniques, and post-harvest processing, thus making standardization difficult. Herbs are regulated by the Food and Drug Administration (FDA), but differently than prescription medications. With this lack of close oversight, herbs can vary immensely in their components. With approximately half of the herbs taken by patients not reported to their physicians, there is significant potential for interactions with prescription medications and nonprescription substances *(18)*.

AYURVEDA

Another non-Western whole medical system is Ayurveda. Developed by Brahmin sages some 5000 years ago in India, *Ayurveda* literally means knowledge of life. As this suggests, it is a health care approach beyond the mere treatment of disease, one whose fundamental principle is the integration of mind, body, and spirit. Various techniques are utilized to achieve this integration including diet, herbal therapy, aromatherapy, cleansing rituals, meditation, and yoga. Ayurveda is still practiced actively today as an integral part of the Indian health care system. As in TCM, the concept of balance is a fundamental principle of Ayurveda. Each individual, as part of the natural rhythm, is influenced by three fundamental universal energies: the three doshas—Vata, Pitta, and Kapha. These three elements are present in every human cell, tissue, and organ, and vary according to the individual's unique constitution. Imbalances of these doshas can lead to disease and suffering. Ayurveda strives to balance these doshas, which are influenced by diet, seasons, lifestyle, genetic tendencies, and the like. Diagnosis performed by a certified practitioner relies heavily on tongue and pulse analysis, which help determine the individual's constitution and identify imbalances. Herbal preparations, dietary instructions, and lifestyle advice are all provided to rebalance the individual's unique constitution.

Meditation, yoga, and breathing techniques are the foundation of ayurvedic therapies. Panchakarma, a series of cleansing rituals, is frequently employed to rid the body of impurities and therefore to rebalance the doshas. Increasingly more research studies on ayurvedic principles are beginning to emerge, but thus far most of the research on Ayurveda coming out of India generally falls short of contemporary methodological standards. A

recent article in *JAMA* studied several OTC ayurvedic preparations sold in the Boston area and discovered a disturbingly high
percentage contained toxic chemicals such as lead, mercury, and
arsenic *(19)*. This most likely represents poor-quality manufacturing techniques, rather than flawed fundamental health care
principles and practices.

Western Systems

Two other whole medical systems have evolved in the West:
homeopathy and napropathy.

HOMEOPATHY

Homeopathy, derived from the Greek *homoeo* (similar) and
patho (disease) was developed by an 18th-century German physician, Samuel Hahnemann. However, its historical roots claim
to date back to Hippocrates and Indian healers. The fundamental
concept of homeopathy is the principle of similars: "like cures
like," that is, substances that produce the same symptoms of a
disease can be used to cure that disease. For example, if the symptoms of a respiratory infection were similar to the symptoms of
mercury poisoning, then mercury would be the homeopathic
remedy for that infection. The homeopathic substance, in this
example, mercury, is called the simillium. The mercury is not
administered directly, but first treated through a series of dilu-
tions, sometimes as dilute as one part to 1 billion. This concept,
called potentiation, contends that the more dilute the remedy, the
more potent the cure. The diluent, such as water, would then retain
"trace memory" of the initial substance.

Homeopathy also proposes the concept of the single remedy; no matter how many symptoms one manifests only one remedy is taken and that remedy will affect all those symptoms.
Because homeopathy is administered in extremely dilute, minute,
or potentially nonexistent doses, there is significant skepticism
on the part of conventional medicine. Homeopathic practitioners
claim, however, that this approach is similar to allergy medicine

or the use of vaccines; in both techniques a small amount of substance is administered to bolster the immune system against that disease. Because homeopathic remedies are taken in such minute doses, they appear to be safe. Homeopaths claim this approach is much more specific than conventional medicine, based on highly individualized treatments, and hence difficult to study using conventional, clinical trial methods.

NAPROPATHY

Sometimes referred to as naprapathy and considered a universal healing system, napropathy was developed in the late 1800s by Dr. Oakley Smith. A chiropractor himself, Dr. Smith was disappointed that chiropractic techniques only provided fleeting relief for his back pain, and through his research discovered the importance and healing potential of manipulating the soft tissue between the bones. Through experimentation and assimilation of various healing techniques, he developed the field of napropathy. Napropathy emphasizes health restoration and maintenance as well as disease prevention. Today, naprapaths see a broader range of conditions than say, for example, chiropractors or massage therapists. They treat such problems as anxiety, depression, fatigue, skin conditions, and menopausal symptoms *(20)*. There are six fundamental principles of napropathy, which will appear similar to other systems of health care:

1. The healing power of nature.
2. Identification and treatment of the cause of the disease.
3. "First do no harm."
4. The doctor as teacher.
5. Treatment of the whole person.
6. Prevention *(2)*.

Perhaps more than other whole medical systems, napropathy seems to integrate and utilize a wide variety of healing approaches such as nutritional supplements, herbal medicines, acupuncture and Chinese medicine, homeopathy, hydrotherapy, massage and joint manipulation, and lifestyle counseling, while tapping into the healing power within the body that establishes, maintains, and restores health. There are no studies available on napropathy as a complete system of medicine.

Summary of Alternative Medicine

When viewed together, there is an underlying theme that permeates these whole medical system practices; a theme of the natural order of the body, supported by a vital energy, a life force, or a balance that when interrupted or distorted causes disease or dysfunction. Through various techniques, the goal of these systems is to restore the natural balance of the system by tapping into or unblocking the obstructed natural flow of a subtle, unmeasurable life force or energy. Balance is maintained through ongoing, often daily, pactices.

As these concepts are either foreign to conventional medicine or unable to be better defined and/or measured in scientific terms, conventional medicine is skeptical not only of the practices themselves, but any purported benefits that may arise. Unfortunately, few well-designed, well-controlled scientific research studies have been completed on these systems to either support or disclaim proponents' experiences and testimonials. Fortunately, as was the case with the recent studies on acupuncture and osteoarthritis, more well-designed studies are ongoing that will stand up to scientific scrutiny and perhaps widen not only the medical armamentarium, but expand the understanding of physiology and the mechanisms of health and disease.

Mind–Body Interventions

Mind–body interventions represented a major portion of the complementary and alternative techniques used in the United States in 2002. Relaxation techniques, imagery, biofeedback, and hypnosis were used by more than 30% of the US population *(2)*.

Ancient health care systems such as TCM and Ayurveda recognize the relationship between mind and body and the importance of both approaches in the healing process—an approach prevalent today. These systems of medicine view illness as an opportunity for personal growth and transformation, beyond just the cure of the disease.

Hippocrates also recognized the spiritual aspects of healing, but as a more reductionist approach to modern medicine developed, the mind–body connection became less important. The focus changed to biology and physiology, cells, bacteria, viruses, and those entities that could be measured and observed. This dichotomy continues today, although recent investigations like those of Walter Cannon in the 1920s and the work of Hans Selye have begun to bridge the gap between emotion, thought, and the corresponding physiological responses. Cannon coined the concept "fight or flight" and defined the corresponding physiological, sympathetic, and adrenal activations in the face of perceived danger. Dr. Selye went on to describe in detail the concept of stress; the nonspecific physiological response of the body to any demand placed on it *(21,22)*.

Understanding there is a physiological, measurable response to cognition has caused a resurgence of the mind–body connection in conventional medicine. With the placebo effect well recognized in modern medicine, better understanding this connection may prove worthwhile to patients. The myriads of mind–body techniques strive to incorporate just that. These techniques involve a wide range of therapies including relaxation, hypnosis, visual imagery, meditation, yoga, biofeedback, Tai Chi, Qi Qong, cognitive–behavior therapy, group support, autogenic training, spirituality, and prayer. Research is beginning to emerge in this field in areas such as pain control, headache, low back pain, effect on the immune system, wound healing, the placebo effect and surgical preparation of patients *(2)*.

Meditation is one of the more popular and publicly available mind–body techniques. Typically thought of as a self-help or personal growth technique, meditation has been evaluated in numerous scientific studies. Probably the most widely researched technique is the transcendental meditation (TM) program. With more than 500 scientific studies on the technique in the areas of physiology, psychology, sociology, education, and rehabilitation, and with articles in prestigious journals such as *Science, Hypertension, American Journal of Physiology*, and *Scientific American*, TM is certainly one of the most intensively study techniques in the field of human development today. Canter recently reviewed the literature on numerous meditative techniques, including TM, and although he found benefits with the technique in areas such as hypertension, he found the current evidence for the therapeutic effects of any type of meditation to be weak, although he points out future trials with improved design may provide concrete, positive benefits *(23,24)*. Other papers have also reviewed cognitive–behavioral techniques such as biofeedback, relaxation, and meditation specifically for the treatment of hypertension, and identified the limited quality literature available on the subject, mainly owing to methodology inadequacies *(25)*.

Biologically Based Therapies

Biologically based therapies include a wide range of substances such as vitamins, minerals, botanicals, animal derived extracts, proteins, amino acids, prebiotics, probiotics, dietary supplements, whole diets, and functional foods. All one need do is visit a health food store to view the plethora of available biologically based therapies. In 2002, an estimated $18.7 billion was spent on dietary supplements alone, with herbs/botanical supplements accounting for approx $4.3 billion in sales *(2)*. About 22% of the population use biologically based therapies, and about 19% use natural products, including Echinacea, ginseng, ginkgo biloba, garlic supplements, glucosamine, St. Johns Wort, peppermint, fish oil, ginger supplements, and soy supplements. As previously noted, given the fact that many patients do not tell their physicians about the use of these substances, and that many patients use these in combination with prescription drugs and other substances, the potential for drug–drug interactions is high.

Dietary supplements are regulated differently than drug products (either prescription medications or OTC medications) by the FDA, without the level of pre- and postmarketing surveillance required for prescription medications. If a biologically based substance such as an herb, vitamin, or mineral is used to resolve a nutrition deficiency or to improve the function of the body, it is considered a dietary supplement. If it is used to prevent, treat, or cure a disease, it is considered a drug. Although required to be safe, there are no specific guidelines on what can be labeled and marketed as a specific product. In other words, if one looks for "fish oil," there are numerous varieties of fish oil available, in various combinations, as no defined standards exist. As with other aspects of CAM, the research on these biologically based therapies is fraught with methodological problems, quality control, and definitional issues. Given the already established, extensive market penetration of these substances, it is not surprising that there is a lack of enthusiasm by producers to expose their products to rigorous, scientific scrutiny.

With numerous OTC preparations available and so many patients using them, one obvious concern is potential drug interactions. Several cases have been reported of increased bleeding associated with gingko biloba when used with anticoagulant or antiplatelet medications, whereas dietary supplements such as garlic, glucosamine, ginseng, sal palmetto, soy, and yohimbe have been shown to either interfere or potentiate prescription medications, or have their own isolated toxicities *(26)*. A recent, systematic review found high-dose vitamin E may actually increase mortality, whereas several trials (e.g., the Heart Protection trial) have shown less than beneficial effects of vitamin therapy *(27– 29)*.

Chelation is a unique alternative treatment, somewhat different than other biologically based therapies. A technique that infuses ethylenediamineteraacetic acid intravenously, chelation has been used therapeutically in situations where cations such as lead, magnesium, zinc, iron, or calcium are in excess. Chelation is now being used to remove calcium from atheromatous plaques. The theory goes that as calcium is removed, atherosclerosis will reverse, resulting in improved coronary and peripheral blood flow. Therapy is usually provided over multiple sessions, both to treat vascular disease and to prevent its occurrence. Although figures vary, data from 1993 estimated more than 500,000 patients per year were treated in the United States with chelation therapy, with financial estimates on its cost at greater than $400 million per year *(30)*. By 1997, more than 800,000 patient visits were made for chelation therapy. A 2002 paper published the results of a randomized trial of chelation therapy in patients with ischemic heart disease and found no benefits in terms of the time to ischemia, exercise capacity, or quality of life *(31)*. Currently, the NIH is conducting a randomized, controlled trial on the potential benefits of chelation in heart disease. This is another example of a therapy that perhaps has a theoretical foundation, but lacks efficacy data.

Manipulative and Body-Based Therapies

Manipulative and body-based therapies are those practices that focus primarily on the bones, joints, soft tissues, the circulatory and lymphatic systems. Although these treatments are a fundamental component of ancient health care systems, many have been developed and popularized more recently. There are numerous practices that fall into this category including chiropractic, craniosacral treatments, reflexology, acupressure, and Rolfing, to name just a few. Visits to chiropractors and massage therapists alone account for approx 50% of all visits to CAM practitioners *(7)*. Common principles among these therapies are the beliefs that the human body is self-regulating, all aspects are interrelated, and the body is capable of healing itself. Many of these types of techniques, although not widely accepted by conventional medicine, are more easily understood by physicians and patients, particularly body manipulation and massage techniques especially when used for isolated "mechanical" problems such as musculoskeletal or back pain.

Chiropractic is certainly the most recognizable of all the manipulative therapies. It is the largest, most regulated and best recognized of the CAM treatments that have traditionally functioned outside mainstream medicine *(32)*. Chiropractors are visited more frequently in the United States than any other alternative provider. Although spinal manipulation, the hallmark of chiropractic, is one of the oldest, most widely used and practiced method of manipulative therapies, modern chiropractic dates itself to 1895 when developed by Daniel Palmer. Palmer developed the concept of "innate intelligence," the natural healing ability of the body, and integrated this idea with conventional knowledge of anatomy and physiology. He was a proponent of natural healing—he espoused the avoidance of drugs and surgery as unnatural and focused more on what he perceived as the normal functioning of the nervous system as the key to health.

Palmer believed neurological dysfunction developed as the result of impinged nerves at the level of the spine and that spinal manipulation (adjustments) removed these impingements and allowed normal functioning of the system. This adjustment is achieved by the application of a force to a specific body part, through various techniques, with therapeutic intent. Most chiropractors, however, have expanded their practices and also work with other modalities such as the application of heat, cold, electrical methods, massage, as well as nutritional and lifestyle counseling, vitamin therapy, relaxation techniques, and so on. Chiropractors are also one of the few groups of CAM practitioners that utilize modern diagnostic techniques such as X-rays.

Perhaps one of the appeals of chiropractic is the "hands-on," high-touch, low-tech approach. Chiropractic is very patient-centered and less disease-focused than conventional medicine. Numerous randomized trials have studied the benefits of chiropractic for acute, subacute, and chronic low back pain. These studies have shown at least moderate success in this area *(33)*. However, systematic data are lacking on the overall benefits of chiropractic.

Energy Therapies

Energy therapies are perhaps the most esoteric of all the CAM practices. These can be divided into two types: veritable (those that can be measured) and putative (those that cannot or have not been measured).

Veritable Energy Therapies

Veritable (measurable) energies include sound and electromagnetic forces including visible light, magnetism, and monochromatic radiation. There are many well-established uses of measurable energies in conventional medicine as well, from both a diagnostic and therapeutic perspective. MRI, cardiac pacemakers, electrocardiograms, radiation therapy, ultraviolet light for psoriasis, and laser keratoplasty are common examples. Magnet therapy, popular today for musculoskeletal and arthritic pain, has been used for centuries. Television and print ads are resurrecting many of these therapies supported by testimonials and claims of dramatic improvements. Research is now beginning to uncover the physiological responses of many of these therapies.

Pulse electromagnetic therapy has been used for years in orthopedic injuries and to accelerate healing fractures. Sound wave therapy, such as music therapy, has also been used for years for pain and anxiety, either alone or in combination with imagery. Even the most skeptical among us can vouch for, from personal experience, the beneficial effects of sound therapy (music). Light therapy has been well documented to impact seasonal affective disorders, with less effective data on depression and sleep disorders. When viewed in their proper context, energy therapies are a well-established component of conventional medicine as well as CAM, widely used, and with multiple applications.

Putative Energy Therapies

What are more interesting in the context of this chapter are the putative (yet-to-be measured) energy therapies. An underlying theme in many CAM practices is the concept of a vital force, an inherent natural energy that permeates the individual and maintains health and wellness. This energy has various names; qi (TCM), the doshas in ayurvedic medicine, innate intelligence, creative intelligence/transcendental consciousness, and the like, but the fundamental principle is the same; tapping into or allowing this energy to flow unimpeded will cure disease, support the physiology, and perhaps result in personal and spiritual growth. Because this energy cannot be measured by current techniques, verifying the effects of these practices is difficult. All one can do is quantify and measure presumed outcomes or effects of these methods, which is not all that dissimilar to some aspects of conventional medicine. Various medications we use or therapies we employ have specific benefits, but the exact mechanisms of action are unknown.

Conventional medicine also relies on the "healing power of nature." Immobilization is the most common treatment for fractures—letting nature heal the break. The pH of the stomach, the coagulation and thrombolytic systems, as well as the immune systems are all examples of what a CAM practitioner would consider the healing power of nature. Energy therapies aim to better tap into this natural order and direct this healing power of nature in a more specific manner. Acupuncture, herbal medicine, meditation, yoga, Qi Gong, and homeopathy are examples of treatments aimed to influence or unblock this healing biofield. Some methods use a practitioner to either directly touch the individual or merely pass their hands over the patient to strengthen or rejuvenate the patient's energy. These include, for example, therapeutic touch, Reiki, vortex healing, and polarity healing. Distant healing proponents claim this energy can be redirected from a distance and does not even require personal contact with the patient.

Perhaps the most obvious example of "distant healing" would fall under the category of prayer. As noted in the NIH 2002 survey, prayer specifically for health reasons was the most commonly used CAM therapy employed; intercessory prayer (prayer for another) was also common.

Certainly the "mechanism" of prayer is immeasurable, but research studies are ongoing investigating its overall effectiveness. Attempts have also been made to measure these energy fields, in particular electromagnetic fields, but today no specific, quantifiable data arc available.

A SYSTEMATIC APPROACH TO CAM

This chapter has discussed many of the diverse practices that comprise CAM. With the multiple techniques, philosophies, and types of CAM available, a systematic structural framework was called for to better understand, investigate, legitimize, and disseminate information on CAM. This much needed, major initiative was undertaken in 1992, when Congress established within the NIH the Office of Alternative Medicine to investigate and evaluate promising, unconventional medical practices. With an initial budget of $2 million, the Office of Alternative Medicine sponsored workshops on alternative medicinal practices and developed an infrastructure to provide grant money for rescarch into CAM. Its first phase III clinical trial was funded in 1997, a study of St. John's Wort for major depression.

By 1998, Congress established the NCCAM by elevating the status of the Office of Alternative Medicine to that of an NIH center. The NCCAM is dedicated to exploring complementary and alternative practices through rigorous scientific study, to provide training of CAM researchers, and to make authoritative information on CAM available to the public and health care professionals. The four primary focus areas of the NCCAM—research, research training and career development, outreach, and integration—are supported by a yearly budget of now more than $123 million. Recent publications in mainstream medical journals are a direct result of NCCAM funding *(2)*. An interesting and very important role of the center is the integration of scientifically proven studies on CAM practices into conventional medicine by announcing public research results, investigating ways to better integrate evidence-based CAM practices into conventional medical practices, and supporting programs intended to incorporate CAM into the curriculum of medical, dental, and nursing schools. These principles were the foundation of the first 5-year plan of the NCCAM, "Expanding Horizons of Heath Care" *(2)*.

In addition to the work of the NCCAM, mainstream medical publications such as *The New England Journal of Medicine, JAMA*, and *The Archives of Internal Medicine* have developed an interest in CAM. The *Annals of Internal Medicine* sponsored and published an extensive, extremely well-structured series of articles on CAM, many referenced within this chapter *(34)*. Numerous "alternative" periodicals now exist providing health care practitioners of all persuasions information on the historical foundation of CAM practices, methodologies, uses, and evidence-based outcomes. There are numerous ongoing clinical trials, many through the support of the NCCAM, in areas such as chelation therapy for heart disease, biofeedback for hypertension, CAM approaches to menopause, affective and anxiety disorders, multiple sclerosis, and the use of probiotics to treat infectious disease, just to name a few.

Why such an effort to develop evidence-based data on CAM? Many of these therapies have been used for thousands of years, why invest the time and money "verifying" what people have continued to use, presumably because they are working? If these therapies have stood the test of time, why open Pandora's Box? It seems the most common criticism of CAM practices is the lack of evidence on their effectiveness. The foundation of conventional medicine is the scientific method. Advances in conventional medicine are based on rigorous, scientific research, as well as the ongoing application of scientific and statistical methods in order to make available to patients those therapies that have proven most beneficial. Interestingly, one of the first evidence-based studies found in the literature involved what might be considered an alternative therapy today, "high-dose" vitamin therapy in the form of lemon juice to prevent scurvy on British naval vessels.

However, much of conventional medicine is often based on experience rather than hard data. With clinical variability and patient individuality, it is difficult, if not impossible, to study every drug or every procedure in every varied situation. Extrapolation is necessary. This does not, however, allow the provision of medical services, either as conventional medicine or CAM, without the responsibility of systematic review and oversight of treatments that are made available and marketed to the general public. Marketing styles today and the media messages with which the general public are constantly bombarded often contain explicit claims that have little, if any, validity.

Modern health care, both conventional medicine and CAM, must submit to scientific study and oversight, using the best available research and statistical methodologies, not only to gain credibility, but to help determine what practices truly benefit our patients, despite our biases or predilections. Not only do we need to better understand what works, but how better to disseminate that information to practitioners to assure our patients receive the benefit of that knowledge. Despite evidence-based outcomes for numerous clinical scenarios-data shows practitioners still do not always provide those proven therapies or medications to their patients on a consistent basis, despite well-researched, well-publicized national guidelines. Developing and defining best practices is one thing—getting practitioners to follow these guidelines is another.

Perhaps another reason physicians are hesitant to embrace CAM is the lack of understanding or believability of the proposed mechanisms of action. Even with conventional medicine, mechanisms of action are not fully delineated or explained, but they are more within the profession's realm of understanding. Although exact pathways or receptor effects of various medications are not well understood, we know they affect and influence known and accepted physiological mechanisms. Even the placebo effect, well researched and well documented in conventional medicine, is still not well understood. To begin to accept "universal life force" or "vital energy" as the medium of healing, while conventional medicine is unable to measure, define or quantify these entities, to many physicians is reminiscent of the days of snake oil and seen as taking a giant step backward.

What makes this more difficult are the problems associated with applying the scientific method to many CAM practices. Controlled trails are difficult to design for chiropractic, acupuncture, acupressure, or therapeutic touch. Homeopathy is a very individualized therapy; what works for one person probably will not work for another. Herbal products are not well regulated and therefore there is a lack of uniformity in definition and quality control. Modern science often searches for and isolates the active ingredient in a preparation and then studies the biological effects of that ingredient: in CAM the whole plant is often used as it is thought to offset potential side effects—the whole being more that the sum of its parts.

Still another question remains: what is legitimate healing? *(35)*. Is healing an improvement over one's baseline condition, or it is an improvement over and above what one might attribute to the placebo effect? If, as this intimates, patients have used CAM for centuries with only subjective improvement, is this sufficient evidence of success? Must improvement fall within our measurable, defined, scientific methodological paradigms? It seems the cultural, politically dominant system of the time defines that paradigm, such as the scientific model. For centuries, Ayurveda and TCM were well respected and flourished within their cultures, with explanations such as the balancing of doshas or unblocking qi, explanations well understood and accepted in those cultures. Were the benefits patients experienced any less legitimate?

Are there risks in embracing CAM? Certainly, malpractice and liability concerns are to be considered (and are discussed in a later chapter). With many physicians now providing CAM therapies within their offices, these issues must be addressed. Hospitals are now faced with new dilemmas, such as how to credential alternative practices where little data are available to assess the effectiveness of these practices, or to assess the competence of the practitioners. Hospitals can rely on already established state licensure policies, but are still faced with how to offer these services in the traditional, conventional medicine environment.

Not only have numerous articles been written on the lack of benefit of certain CAM therapeutic approaches, but also on the ethics and legalities of encouraging patients to use these therapies at the expense of proven modalities. Recommending alternative therapies over well-proven therapies, such as cancer chemotherapies, is certainly fraught with problems. However, conventional medicine must guard against unilaterally dismissing CAM, otherwise many potential benefits for patients may be missed.

There are many lessons physicians can learn from CAM. Prevention, health maintenance, doctor–patient interactions and communication, and chronic disease and pain management are all areas on which conventional medicine could improve. Mechanisms of action are less important to patients than to physicians. Patients want to get better or maintain health and well-being, however defined or measured. Consumer preference will dictate what types of care will be available. The market will then provide what patients want or need. The fact that more patients visit CAM practitioners than primary care physicians bears witness *(7)*. This is a movement that is centuries old, and growing.

Contemporary medicine can seem to discount the body's own natural healing abilities. Perhaps CAM can be a vehicle to assist in a better understanding scientifically of what these healing powers are and how they can be tapped into. Contemporary medicine requires an understanding that fits its current paradigms, rather than recreating or redefining those models to fit the data. For example, several studies show positive results of homeopathy but by scientific principles, these effects should not be seen—so adherents of conventional medicine disbelieve the evidence *(36)*.

CAM is often not accepted because it is culturally different, because mechanisms are not clearly understood or are explained in a way that is contrary to our belief system or currently accepted medical and scientific concepts. Modern medicine requires an understanding that fits its current constructs. CAM challenges these paradigms, and perhaps will facilitate a paradigm shift. This shift will only occur when data is unequivocal, hence the need for well-designed, repeatable trials to determine what does and does not work. CAM must be willing to undergo this study and to stand up to scientific scrutiny.

Conventional medicine is not without issues, either. Scientific research has its flaws—medications once thought safe are now found not to be so. Scientific knowledge must be adaptable when the results are unequivocal—conventional medicine must be willing to incorporate those techniques when proven beneficial for patients. Similarly, CAM must be willing to put aside practices proven unfounded in scientific, controlled trials. Galileo was ostracized when his views contradicted the current political, religious, and scientific standards. Let us not do the same when proven knowledge can benefit others. If outcomes are clear, perhaps clearly understanding mechanisms is less important.

As the understanding of CAM practices advances, an integration of conventional medicine and those proven CAM practices will certainly occur. Perhaps this was best stated by Fontanarosa and Lundberg:

> There is no alternative medicine. There is only scientifically proven, evidence based medicine supported by solid data or unproven medicine, for which scientific evidence is lacking. Whether a therapeutic practice is "eastern" or "western," is unconventional or mainstream, or involves mind–body techniques, or molecular genetics is largely irrelevant except for historical purposes and cultural interest.... We must focus on fundamental issues—mainly, the target disease or condition, the proposed treatment and the need for convincing data on safety and therapeutic efficacy. *(37)*

Only then can we blend the best that both conventional medicine and CAM have to offer.

REFERENCES

1. Lowes, R. CAM practitioner on board? Medical Economics November 19, 2004;22–26.
2. National Center for Complementary and Alternative Medicine. Available at: http://nccam.nih.gov Accessed on February 6, 2005.
3. Defining and Describing Complementary and Alternative Medicine. CAM Research Methodology Conference, April 1995. Alternative Therapies 1997;3(2):49–57.
4. Eisenberg DM, Kessler RC, Foster C, Norlock FE, Calkins DR, Delbanco TL. Unconventional medicine in the United States. Prevalence, costs, and patterns of use. N Engl J Med 1993;328: 246–252.
5. Renner J. HealthSmarts. Kansas City, MO: HealthFacts, 1990.
6. Kaptchuk TJ, Eisenberg DM. Varieties of healing. 1: medical pluralism in the United States. Ann Intern Med 1998;135(3): 189–195.

7. Eisenberg DM, Davis RB, Ettner SL, et al. Trends in alternative medicine use in the United States, 1990–1997. JAMA 1998;280:1569–1575.
8. Kaptchuk TJ, Eisenberg DM. Long term trends in the use of complementary and alternative therapies in the United States. Ann Intern Med 2001;135(4):262–268.
9. Barnes PM, Powell-Grimes E, McFann K, Nahin RL. Complementary and alternative medicine use among adults: United States, 2002. U.S. Department of Health and Human Services. Advanced Data May 27, 2004; 343.
10. Rao JK, Mihaliak K, Kroenke K, Bradley J, Tierney WM, Weinberger M. Use of complementary therapies for arthritis among patients of rheumatologists. Ann Intern Med 1999;131(6):409–416.
11. Eisenberg DM, Kessler RC, Van Rompay MI, et al. Perceptions about complementary therapies relative to conventional therapies among adults who use both: results from a national survey. Ann Intern Med 2001;135(5):344–351.
12. Kaptchuk TJ, Eisenberg DM. The persuasive appeal of Alternative medicine. Ann Intern Med 1998;129(12):1061–1065.
13. Eisenberg DM. Advising patients who seek alternative medical therapies. Ann Intern Med 1997;127(1):61–69.
14. Davidoff, F. Weighing the alternatives. Lessons from the paradoxes of alternative medicine. Ann Intern Med 1999;129(12):1068–1070.
15. Jonas WB, Levin JS (eds.). Essentials of complementary and alternative medicine. Baltimore, MD:Lippincott, Williams & Wilkins, 1999.
16. Kaptchuk TJ. Acupuncture: theory, efficacy, and practice. Ann Intern Med 2002;136(5):374–383.
17. Berman BM, Lao L, Langenberg P, Lee WL, Gilpin AMK, Hochberg MC. Effectiveness of acupuncture as adjunctive therapy in osteoarthritis of the knee: a randomized controlled trial. Ann Intern Med 2004;141(12):901–910.
18. Foster DF, Phillips RS, Hamel MB, Eisenberg DM. Alternative medicine use in older Americans. J Am Geriatr Soc 2000;48:1560–1565.

19. Saper RB, Stefanos KN, Paquin J, et al. Heavy metal content of ayurvedic herbal medicine products. JAMA 2004;292(23): 2868–2873.

20. Cherkin DC, Deyo RA, Sherman KJ, et al. Characteristics of visits to licensed acupuncturists, chiropractors, massage therapists, and naturopathic physicians. J Am Board Fam Pract 2002;15: 463–472.

21. Cannon WB. The wisdom of the body. New York: Norton,1932.

22. Selye H. The stress of life. New York: McGraw-Hill, 1956.

23. Schneider RH, Staggers F, Alexander CN, et al. A randomized controlled trial of stress reduction for hypertension in older African Americans. Hypertension 1995;26:820–827.

24. Canter PH. The therapeutic effects of meditation. BMJ 2003;326: 1049–1050.

25. Eisenberg DM, Delbanco TL, Berkey CS, et al. Cognitive behavioral techniques for hypertension. Ann Intern Med 1993;118(12): 964–972.

26. De Smet PA. Herbal remedies. N Engl J Med 2002;347(25): 2046–2056.

27. Hercberg S, Galan P, Preziosi P, et al. The SU.VI.MAX Study. Arch Intern Med 2004;164:2335–2342.

28. Miller ER, Barriuso R, Darshan D, Rei Mersma RA, Appel LJ, Guallar E. Meta-analysis: high-dose vitamin E supplementation may increase all-cause mortality. Ann Intern Med 2005;142(1): 37–46.

29. MRC/BHF Heart Protection Study of Cholesterol Lowering with Simvastatin in 20,536 High-Risk Individuals: A Randomized Placebo-Controlled Trial. Lancet 2002;360:7–22.

30. Grier MT, Meyers DG. So much writing, so little science: a review of 37 years of literature on edetate sodium chelation therapy. Ann Pharmacother 1993;27:1504–1509.

31. Knudtson ML, Wyse DG, Galbraith PD, et al. Chelation therapy for ischemic heart disease. JAMA 2002;287(4):481–486.

32. Meeker WC, Haldeman S. Chiropractic: a profession at the crossroads of mainstream and alternative medicine. Ann Intern Med 2002;136(3):216–227.

33. Koes BW, Assendelft WJ, Van der Heijden GJ, Bouter LM. Spinal manipulation for low back pain. An updated systematic review of randomized clinical trials. Spine 1996;21:2860–2871.
34. Eisenberg DM, Kaptchuk TJ, Laine C, Davidoff F. Complementary and alternative medicine—an annals series. Ann Intern Med 2001;135(3):208.
35. Kaptchuk TJ. The placebo effect in alternative medicine: can the performance of a healing ritual have a clinical significance? Ann Intern Med 2002;136(11):817–825.
36. Vanderbroucke JP, deCrean AJ. Alternative medicine: a "mirror image" for scientific reasoning in conventional medicine. Ann Intern Med 2001;135(7):507–513.
37. Fontanarosa PB, Lundberg GD. Alternative medicine meets science. JAMA 1998;280:1618–1619.

3

Complementary and Alternative Medicine

The Physician's Ethical Obligations

Wayne Vaught, PhD

INTRODUCTION

Cynthia Langley was in her 32nd week of pregnancy. She had met with all but one of her obstetricians and was excited about the birth of her first child. At first she considered using a midwife, but none were covered by her insurance plan and she felt more secure with her physician. Nonetheless, Ms. Langley had certain expectations. Even without a midwife, she wanted a natural birth. She drafted a birth plan, reviewing it carefully with each physician during her prenatal visits. She also employed the services of a doula, a birthing assistant, to provide constant support and assist with nonconventional birthing techniques during labor.

Ms. Langley's physicians were encouraging and generally agreeable with her plans. Some even described positive experiences with the use of a doula. One physician, after being ques-

From: *Biomedical Ethics Reviews: Complementary and Alternative Medicine: Ethics, the Patient, and the Physician*
Edited by: L. Snyder © Humana Press Inc., Totowa, NJ

tioned about the safety and efficacy of caster oil as a nonconventional means to induce labor, which her doula recommended, provided Ms. Langley with the recipe for a "caster-oil root beer float." Another physician, however, suggested that the doula, who would not be covered by insurance, was possibly a waste of money. "It's up to you," he said, "but there are certainly other things that I would spend my money on." Although disappointed by the comment, Ms. Langley was undeterred. Her doula was very supportive and she wanted someone to be at her side throughout her labor.

Ms. Langley's pregnancy was uneventful and she felt comfortable with her physicians. Unfortunately, all this changed during her final scheduled prenatal visit. She met with Dr. Morris, the one physician in the practice with whom she had not yet met. When she asked if he had seen her birth plan he smiled and suggested that she had been reading too much. He seemed unimpressed with her preparations for labor. When she asked about his experiences with a doula, he tried to reassure her that everything was under control. Her plans, and especially the doula, were unnecessary and quite possibly intrusive. "We've been trained to do this," he explained, "you should trust that we know what to do." He clearly did not like the idea of a patient planning her impending delivery.

Ms. Langley was not relieved by his reassurances. She feared that Dr. Morris would be on call when she delivered. Although his partners had been supportive, he belittled her birthing plans and challenged the appropriateness of a doula. As the days passed, her attention increasingly focused on Dr. Morris and her fear that he would ruin her birth experience.

Was Dr. Morris right? Did he respond appropriately to Ms. Langley's desire to integrate a doula?

Growing numbers of Americans utilize practices frequently referred to, in the United States, as complementary and alternative medicine (CAM). CAM therapies include a wide range of treatment modalities, ranging from ancient Chinese practices to chiropractic and massage therapies. In May 2004 the Centers for

Disease Control reported that 36% of Americans utilized some form of CAM *(1,1a,1b)*. When prayer was included, the number rose to 62%. Furthermore, it is estimated that Americans spent as much as $47 billion on CAM in 1997. Of this expenditure, as much as $19.6 billion was paid out of pocket. This represents more than was paid out of pocket for all hospital expenses and about half of what was paid out of pocket for all physician services *(1,1a,1b)*. Consequently, as patients increasingly seek to integrate CAM modalities into conventional therapy, they raise significant practical and ethical challenges for physicians.

As Ms. Langley discovered, attitudes among physicians toward the use of CAM are quite diverse, ranging from those who encourage or even utilize some forms of CAM to those who are more skeptical and discouraging. What are a physician's ethical obligations when confronted with CAM? How should physicians respond to patients and CAM practitioners who seek to develop an integrative system of health care delivery?

Given the wide range of diverse health care practices that comprise CAM, this chapter does not focus on ethical issues within any particular nonconventional health care system. Rather, it explores the ethical dimensions of care that arise in CAM or integrative medicine. The impetus for such integration is twofold. On the one hand, some physicians, recognizing its therapeutic value, now incorporate selected CAM therapies into their practice. On the other, patients are themselves forcing integration by using CAM in conjunction with conventional medicine. Given the current health care climate, physicians must begin to consider their ethical obligations when caring for patients who use CAM.

WHICH ETHICAL PRINCIPLES ARE APPLICABLE TO CAM?

Before turning to specific ethical obligations, it is useful to consider the moral framework that can most effectively guide health care decision making when physicians encounter CAM. Currently, physicians appear to be headed in one of two directions. Some physicians suggest that the same ethical principles utilized in the context of conventional medicine apply equally well to CAM *(2)*. Proponents of this approach tend to frame the issues related to CAM within the traditional context of autonomy, nonmaleficence, beneficence, and justice *(2–4)*. For example, all physicians, whether they utilize or accommodate CAM in their professional practice, are obliged to help patients make appropriate health care choices (respect autonomy) and to direct patients toward safe and effective alternatives treatment options (beneficence—the duty to promote good and act in the patient's best interest), and avoid doing harm (non-maleficence).

Critics, however, argue that contemporary bioethics is inadequate when considering CAM. Of particular importance is the concern that conventional bioethics fails to take into account the values specific to CAM *(5)*. According to this view, "adopting CAM practices requires a new ethical understanding that incorporates the values implicit in those practices" *(5)*. Accordingly, complementary systems of health care point to the need to develop new theoretical models of ethical decision making *(6)*.

Despite sharp criticisms, critics of conventional bioethics cannot easily dismiss traditional ethical principles. In fact, some proponents of CAM recognize that the principles of autonomy, nonmaleficence, beneficence, and justice raise appropriate concerns related to caregiving *(7)*. Accordingly, contemporary bioethical principles may also play an important role in evaluating CAM *(5)*.

For example, CAM proponents caution that conventional medicine, along with contemporary bioethics, is limited because it lacks a holistic view of the person. Those accepting this view argue that there needs to be more emphasis on culture and spirituality, as they must be taken into account when considering CAM. But are these concerns truly unique to CAM and integrative medicine? Do they point to the need for a new ethical theory?

Or, do they point to important values that have already been raised within the context of conventional medicine?

Not all physicians agree that these values are unique to CAM. Some, in fact, caution that it is a mistake to use the term *holistic* to differentiate between CAM and conventional medicine. Rather, they argue that conventional medicine should also be holistic. Physicians should consider the patient as a whole, and not merely in terms of organs and disease, as healing can be successful only if the patient's mind, body, spirit, community, and culture are taken into account *(2)*. According to this view, a holistic approach to the person is essential in patient care regardless of whether the physician is practicing conventional or nonconventional medicine. Although it is certainly true that physicians may neglect these important issues, it is not clear that the integration of CAM into conventional practice necessitates the need for a new theory of ethics.

Some critics also express concern because they believe contemporary bioethics to have grown out of conventional medicine, arguing that it is merely an imperfect reflection of the values inherent in mainstream medicine *(5)*. However, basic bioethical principles are not specific to conventional health care. In fact, these principles are applicable to a wide range of nonmedical issues. Such broad application gives some physicians assurance as to the usefulness of bioethical principles when evaluating difficult ethical cases in medicine *(2)*.

That contemporary bioethics does not merely reflect the values of conventional medicine should be readily apparent from the wealth of bioethical literature. Much of the literature in bioethics was written by nonphysicians who were not part of the dominant medical culture. More importantly, bioethics has a long history of challenging the values, and accepted cultural practices, of conventional medicine. For example, principle-based bioethics is critical of the tradition of medical paternalism. It also challenges physicians not to view patients merely as biological systems, but to see each patient as a person. It recognizes and emphasizes the importance of the individual and the community in which he or she lives. Ultimately, the need for a bioethical system that is more inclusive of a wide range of beliefs and values has been a central concern in contemporary bioethics.

A more daunting challenge to contemporary bioethics, however, stems from the fact that the dominant system of ethical inquiry in the United States developed out of the Western tradition of thought. Accordingly, bioethics, and its particular principles and ground rules, may ultimately embrace the prevailing cultural values and traditions to the exclusion of non-Western belief systems *(8)*. The principle of autonomy, for example, with its emphasis on independence and self-sufficiency, is foreign to many non-Western cultures. To be responsive to their patient's needs, physicians must recognize such cultural variation regarding who has the authority to make treatment decisions *(8)*. For example, in some cultures it is the family, rather than the individual, that is the locus of decision making in health care. In these cases, it may do considerable harm to impose Western moral values on people who do not share them.

Although physicians should be attentive to culture-specific values when applying the principle of autonomy in patient care, they must be equally careful not to dismiss it entirely when confronting cross-cultural conflicts. Autonomy means literally "self-rule." Yet, conceptions of the self vary across cultures. In cultures where the concept of "individual autonomy" does not exist, physicians must incorporate the patient's culture-specific understanding of the self into treatment decisions. If self-identity is intrinsically tied to a broader understanding of the relationship with one's community, then a more communal approach to treatment decision making may be appropriate.

However, the principle of autonomy, as understood in the West, still holds considerable currency when confronting such conflicts. Suppose, for example, that a female patient comes from a culture that does not recognize individual autonomy. In such a culture, treatment decisions may traditionally rest with the familial patriarch or religious elders. Yet, during an exam, the patient attempts to break with her culture. She informs her physician that she would like to make her own treatment decisions despite objections from her family. Should her request be refused, citing its inconsistency with the dominant beliefs and practices of the culture to which she belongs? To do so would require one to argue that traditional cultural practices should outweigh the value of the patient's own preferences. In this case, the patient's own values would ultimately guide treatment decisions. Nevertheless, respect for patient autonomy, considered broadly and with respect for culture-specific values, can accommodate the wide range of conflicts likely to arise in an integrated health care system.

The utilization of traditional bioethical principles is also evident in the codes of ethics for several CAM professional organizations. For example, the principle of autonomy is reflected in the code of ethics for the American Chiropractic Association (ACA) when it states that its members should recognize the right of every patient of free choice of chiropractors or other health professionals *(9)*. According to the ACA, "doctors of chiropractic should employ their best good faith efforts that the patient possesses enough information to enable an intelligent choice in regard to proposed chiropractic treatment. The patient should make his or her own determination on such treatment" *(9)*. The principle of nonmaleficence is similarly reflected in the code of ethics for the American Association of Naturopathic Physicians. It states that naturopathic physicians shall first strive to do no harm. It acknowledges the worth and dignity of each patient and expects its members to safeguard a patient's right to privacy *(10)*. These codes suggest that some CAM providers rely on traditional bioethical principles, as do physicians, to resolve ethical conflicts that arise in patient care.

The major difficulty with contemporary bioethics when it encounters CAM does not stem from its reliance on widely held ethical principles. Rather, conventional providers encounter problems when they attempt to apply those principles in a rigid fashion. One example of this application of principles can be found in Robert Nash's article "The Biomedical Ethics of Alternative, Complementary, and Integrative Medicine." Here Nash firmly posits four principles as the foundation for ethical discourse, and then proceeds to prioritize them in order of importance *(4)*. Not only does Nash fail to provide a basis for this rigid ordering, the ordering itself is inconsistent with the method proposed by the most prominent advocates of ethical principles *(11)*.

What many proponents of CAM desire, which is consistent with conventional approaches to bioethics, is an open discussion of the competing values underlying widely diverse health care systems and beliefs. In many cases, the values and concerns common to contemporary bioethics will provide a useful guide, as they have proven effective in guiding our ability to answer difficult ethical challenges *(5)*.

DO PHYSICIANS HAVE A DUTY TO LEARN AND ASK ABOUT CAM?

Contemporary bioethical principles are clearly relevant when considering ethical conflicts arising at the intersection of CAM and conventional medicine. Although ethical discourse need not, and in fact should not, be limited to the values expressed by these principles, they do represent a set of widely held values that provide guidance in establishing a physician's ethical obligations regarding integrative medicine. Consider, for example, a physician's obligation to avoid causing unnecessary harm and the obligation to promote patient well-being. Both principles are held widely and have a long and enduring history in medical ethics. But how do these principles translate into specific ethical obligations in regard to CAM?

Such principles establish a basic obligation for physicians to lean about common forms of CAM. Some physicians now realize that they should become sufficiently familiar with common forms of CAM in order to discuss them with their patients. They also recognize the need to identify local CAM providers and to become familiar with their skill and expertise *(2)*. The duty to learn about CAM stems from the generally accepted principles requiring physicians to benefit their patient and to avoid causing harm, beneficence and nonmaleficence. Physicians who are knowledgeable about CAM are going to be better able to promote patient health and to foster more effective patient–physician relationships *(12)*.

The need to learn about common forms of CAM stems from a similar obligation physicians have to understand environmental risks and lifestyle choices. Such knowledge will allow them to more effectively promote patient welfare. For example, physicians should be aware of such environmental risks as smoking, lead, and high-cholesterol diets. They should have some understanding of the sources and symptoms related to these environmental exposures as well as an understanding of how to minimize associated risks. Questions pertaining to lead exposure, for example, are often included as part of a history and physical exam. In addition to collecting this information, physicians should be able to educate patients about potential risks and provide them with useful information and resources.

Physicians must also understand health-promoting lifestyle choices. They must recognize the importance of proper diet, exercise, and social activities that promote both physical and mental well-being. Physicians should be aware of how these practices impact health and provide the patient with enough information to allow them to make informed decisions about their lifestyle preference. They should strive to assist their patients in discovering and incorporating these practices into their daily routine. Physicians who do not take this role seriously ultimately fail in their obligation to promote patient welfare. On the other hand, by helping patients identify both the risks and benefits of their lifestyle choices, physicians will be in a better position to promote positive health outcomes.

As with the impact of other lifestyle choices, CAM will remain a vibrant feature of the American health care landscape. In fact, some commentators note that the health beliefs underlying various CAM modalities are deeply entrenched and are not going to fade away *(8)*. Furthermore, the utilization of CAM does not stem from a lack of education or understanding of science and technology. In fact, many current forms of CAM attract adherents from every ethnicity, social class, and education level *(8)*. Given such widespread and diverse use, physicians must be sufficiently familiar with CAM in order to help their patients understand both its risks and health-promoting benefits.

Not only do physicians have an ethical obligation to learn about CAM, but some nonconventional therapies are becoming so common that physicians may reasonably be accused of negligence for failing to identify and understand them. When physicians readily have access to information regarding the risks and benefits of CAM modalities, they should be aware of that information and be prepared to offer their patients sound advice *(13)*. Lacking understanding, physicians would be unable to help their patients identify important health benefits, or risks, associated with certain CAM modalities. Furthermore, they may run unnecessary tests, or misdiagnose a patient's condition, owing to a lack of familiarity with the common side effects associated with certain CAM treatments.

In addition to the obligation to promote patient welfare, physicians have an obligation to avoid causing unnecessary harm. One growing challenge stems from the fact that many patients are utilizing CAM not as a replacement, but as a supplement to conventional medicine *(14)*. This is particularly important given that some forms of CAM, particularly those utilizing medicinal plants, may interact with conventional pharmaceuticals. One example includes the possible interaction between St. John's Wort and conventional oral contraceptives *(15)*. To provide optimal care, to truly promote their patients' well-being, physicians need to become familiar with common forms of CAM.

Physicians must not only learn about CAM, they must regularly ask patients about it. Two factors should be of concern to physicians. The first, as has been mentioned, is the prevalence of CAM in the general population. In a given practice, several patients may be utilizing some form of CAM in addition to conventional medicine. A high percentage of these patients will not disclose their use of CAM to their physician unless asked. A recent study revealed that 63% of patients integrating CAM and conventional therapy withheld the use of at least one CAM therapy *(16)*. According to these researchers, the most common reasons for nondisclosure include the patient's belief that it is not important for the physician to know and that the physician never asked.

Physicians cannot assume that their patients will alert them to the use of CAM during a routine exam. Even such open-ended questions as "what medications are you currently taking," may fail to elicit information regarding CAM. Some patients may be disinclined to reveal their use of CAM, even when asked. They may be fearful of rejection or simply not recognize the importance of full disclosure. Accordingly, physicians must strive to create a comfortable environment by specifically asking their patients if they are using CAM; and, when they have that information, they should be prepared to use it. In this way, they will be better prepared to meet their patients' informational needs *(13)*. Fortunately, there is also a growing body of research, literature, and clinical tools that provide physicians with relatively easy access to essential information regarding CAM.

It is now well established that physicians have an obligation to promote patient autonomy by providing patients with enough information so that they are able to make well-informed treatment decisions *(13)*. When encountering CAM, physicians need to understand CAM well enough to offer their patients meaningful information. Despite its growing acceptance in mainstream medicine, some physicians argue that their concern for preventing patients from being exposed to unnecessary harms requires

them to steer patients away from CAM. One of the major difficulties with CAM as it currently stands is that it is a broad category that includes a wide range of therapeutic modalities, some
possibly beneficial, some possibly harmful, and some of questionable safety and efficacy. Some well-intentioned physicians,
when asked about CAM, may provide their patients with false or
misleading information, or no information, simply because they
do not understand CAM practices well enough to offer an informed
opinion.

Consider the evaluation offered to Ms. Langley, who ques-
tioned her physician about the role of a doula during her labor.
Although her physicians held a wide range of opinions about the
usefulness of a doula, each admitted to having little knowledge
about the specific skills and services such a person might provide
during labor. None, for example, were aware of the medical literature documenting the health-promoting effects associated with
the inclusion of a doula in the birthing room. For example, patients
utilizing doulas, who offer not only support but may provide massage and touch therapy during labor, are reported to benefit from
shorter labors, fewer epidurals, and decreased need for cesarean
deliveries *(17,18)*. In Ms. Langley's case, at least one physician
introduced an unnecessary level of anxiety for the expectant
mother. Although not life-threatening, the patient's anxiety did
cause some emotional harm.

How should a physician respond to patients who inquire
about CAM? When physicians lack knowledge about the therapy
in question, they should acknowledge their lack of familiarity and
decline to offer a professional opinion for or against its use. When
physicians are unable, or unwilling, to learn about the proposed
treatment, they should recommend that the patient seek out guidance from someone, preferably a colleague, who can offer an educated assessment. Failure to offer a patient such assistance may
subject the patient to the potential risk of fraud or misrepresentation. Accordingly, conscientious physicians who lack an understanding of specific CAM modalities, should attempt to identify

professionals in their community who are familiar with CAM and who can help the patient assess the appropriateness of the specific therapy in question.

Physicians who understand CAM will be in a better position to fulfill their ethical and professional obligations. They will also be better able to promote patient welfare by providing valuable information about the risks and benefits of certain CAM modalities. They will be able to avoid causing harm by identifying possible side effects from CAM use and prevent possible harms from the interaction between CAM and conventional pharmaceuticals. They will also be able to help patients sort through the wide range of CAM options and identify which may by used safely and which should be avoided. In this way, they will be in a better position to foster patient autonomy. The values of autonomy, beneficence, and nonmaleficence clearly highlight a physician's ethical obligation to learn, and ask patients, about CAM.

IS THERE A DUTY TO PROMOTE A CRITICAL EVALUATION OF CAM?

In addition to the duty to learn about CAM and to question patients about its use, physicians should also foster an environment that encourages a fair and thorough evaluation of CAM. At the national level, this duty is beginning to take hold. For example, in 1991 the National Center for Complementary and Alternative Medicine, formerly the Office of Alternative Medicine, was founded to provide a formal mechanism to encourage studies into the efficacy of CAM. Since that time, several studies have shown the efficacy of certain CAM practices for treatment of specific disorders. CAM should continue to be subject to such studies.

Despite encouraging clinical trials, some physicians remain skeptical of most forms of CAM. Although physicians should be concerned about the possibility of harms resulting from the use of CAM, or of patients opting for CAM modalities that are demonstrably ineffective in treating a particular disorder, this is certainly not true of all forms of CAM. Accordingly, in what may seem to some to be an uncertain world of diverse health care practices, it is essential that physicians begin to help their patients and colleagues offer a fair, yet critical analysis of the various forms of CAM.

Discussions of justice in bioethics tend to focus on such issues as the distribution of scarce medical resources. Yet, the principle of justice itself concerns the issue of fairness. Common accounts of justice tend to emphasize such concepts as that which is equitable or owed to persons *(11)*. An injustice, on the other hand, occurs when someone is denied that which they are owed or when they are otherwise treated unfairly *(11)*. Unfair treatment of CAM may deny both patients and CAM providers of certain benefits. Accordingly, justice demands that physicians treat CAM providers in a fair and equitable manner. This section evaluates objections that physicians might encounter related to CAM and considers ways in which physicians can meet their ethical obligations to help patients fairly and accurately evaluate proposed CAM treatment options.

The relationship between what is now considered conventional medicine and CAM has a long and beleaguered history. While striving to place medicine on a scientific foundation and to protect patients from dubious health care practices, physicians have engaged in a longstanding battle with CAM. Early codes of medical ethics, for example, strictly forbade physicians from associating with CAM providers *(5)*. However, such battles tended to focus more on economic considerations than on health care concerns. Presently, the American Medical Association (AMA) code of ethics states that: "it is ethical for a physician to associate professionally with chiropractors provided that the physician believes that such association is in the best interests of his or her patient" *(19)*.

Unfortunately, chiropractic is the only form of CAM mentioned in the AMA code. The omission of other forms of CAM is problematic in that it fails to give equal consideration to other similarly situated CAM modalities. Application of the principle of justice suggests that the AMA code should be revised. This has already occurred in other codes, such as that of the American College of Physicians (ACP), which recognizes that "alternative and complementary health practices are interventions for "improving, maintaining, and promoting health and well-being, preventing disease or treating illnesses, that are not part of a standard North American biomedical regimen of health care or disease prevention" *(20)*. The ACP code goes on to suggest that "requests by patients for alternative treatment require balancing the medical standard of care with a patient's right to choose care on the basis of his or her values and preferences" *(20)*.

Critics vary, in both degree and sophistication, in expressing their concerns about CAM. Some are outspoken opponents of CAM. Others caution that some studies supporting CAM have been so poorly designed or seriously flawed as to provide little useful information about the efficacy of CAM *(21)*. Some argue that there is enough information to determine that many "alternative" treatments are worthless, couching their concerns as a fear that patients may be harmed by turning away from conventional therapies, and toward CAM modalities, which are ineffective *(22)*.

CAM proponents express their concern that many current studies treat non-Western healing systems unfairly because they are "plagued with prejudgments and value-laden terminology" *(8)*. This precludes the possibility of engaging in a fair and useful investigation of the belief systems in question. In some cases,

> pejorative names such as "superstition" (false belief about causal relations, generally involving supernatural or magical implications), "popular errors" (misconceptions among the laity), "old wives' tales" (silly notions, a term that simultaneously derides the tales and their tellers) and "quackery" (properly defined as medical charlatanism involving delib-

erate deception) have sometimes been used as polemical devices intentionally to denigrate the beliefs and practices to which they refer. *(8)*

A prime example of this later tactic, equating CAM with outright quackery, is most prominent in the work of outspoken critics of CAM such as Stephen Barrett. Barrett's attack on CAM is of particular importance because his well known website www.quackwatch.org makes his critique one of the most easily accessible by patients and physicians. Barrett condemns CAM by offering several reasons why patients and physicians should consider most forms of CAM to be nothing more than quackery. He claims CAM therapy is problematic because (a) its rationale or underlying theory has no scientific basis; (b) it has not be demonstrated safe and/or effective by well-designed studies; (c) it is deceptively promoted; or (d) its practitioners are not qualified to make appropriate diagnoses. For these reasons, physicians should not only avoid integrating CAM into conventional care, but should actively discourage their patients from employing CAM modalities *(22)*.

Some of these concerns have been raised by others within the medical community as well. Consider the challenges against CAM services that are deceptively promoted. Undoubtedly, CAM is susceptible to unscrupulous practitioners who may engage in misleading and fraudulent activities. Barrett's infamous website highlights a variety of dubious claims. However, caution must be used in relating these concerns to all forms of CAM. Physicians should familiarize themselves with the developing literature on CAM so that they are better able to distinguish reputable from fraudulent forms of CAM. They also need to help their patients learn to recognize legitimate and illegitimate claims being made by CAM providers. They can meet this latter goal by directing their patients to the growing body of literature that may support certain CAM treatment options.

Although some CAM providers may rightfully be accused of fraud, it is also important to note that misrepresentation is not limited to CAM. Some physicians have been guilty of fraud and misrepresentation. When found guilty, they have been subject to prosecution and loss of their medical license. Accordingly, the principle of justice would encourage physicians to advise their patients to be cautious when considering any treatment, whether it be conventional treatment or CAM, and the credentials of the person offering the service. When encountering CAM, physicians should seek to guide their patients though a fair assessment.

In addition to deception, some physicians are concerned that patients may be harmed by unqualified CAM providers. This too is a legitimate concern. One of the difficulties with some forms of CAM is that it lacks sufficient regulation and oversight to effectively monitor the credentials of alternative providers. In such an environment, there is considerable room for charlatans to simply begin diagnosing and treating without proper training.

But this is not true of all forms of CAM. Some states, for example, do require licensing or registration of certain forms of CAM, such as chiropractic and massage therapy. Additionally, certain forms of CAM, such as acupuncture, chiropractic, naturopathy, and massage therapy, have established training curricula, accredited teaching institutions, and peer-review professional associations that validate credentials. The credentials of individual CAM practitioners can be verified with these organizations. Ensuring that patients seek help from qualified practitioners is a concern for both physicians and CAM providers *(8)*. So, although critics of CAM are right to caution about the risks associated with poorly trained practitioners, it is not a concern unique to CAM nor one that CAM providers fail to acknowledge. Accordingly, physicians may rightfully encourage their patients who are interested in CAM to seek care from qualified practitioners.

Fraud and poorly qualified practitioners raise legitimate concern for any physician attempting to protect a patient's welfare and safety. They are, however, concerns that are applicable to both physicians and CAM providers. Other challenges, however, attack the very nature of certain CAM practices themselves. Some physicians may appeal to these concerns to discount CAM in clinical care. If successful, they could provide legitimate reasons for health care professionals to resist the integration of CAM into conventional therapy. But, do they hold up to further scrutiny? Do these criticisms lead to a fair assessment of CAM? Physicians have an ethical obligation to be aware of these arguments and be prepared to assist their colleagues to recognize their limitations.

Consider, for example, the objection that there is no scientific basis to support the theory behind some forms of CAM. The former editor-in-chief of the *New England Journal of Medicine* expressed this objection. She claims that "healing methods such as homeopathy and therapeutic touch are fervently promoted despite not only the lack of good clinical evidence of effectiveness, but the presence of a rationale that violates fundamental scientific laws" *(23)*. Accordingly, it is not just the lack of studies that concerns her, but the very nature of the practices themselves that deem them unworthy of consideration. She is not alone in expressing such concerns. They were echoed at a 1999 conference on CAM. An attendee of the conference noted that there appeared to be a general consensus that there must be a clearly identifiable biological mechanism to explain the effects of the study. Otherwise, no one would believe it *(24)*. This raises problems for many forms of CAM. According to CAM's critics, "therapeutic touch, homeopathy, moxibustion, and intercessory prayer are examples of practices that are 'preposterous,' and 'impossible' because they lack a plausible biological mechanism" *(24)*.

According to this view, even when studies suggest some therapeutic benefit, the studies themselves should not be taken seriously unless they are accompanied by a plausible biological mechanism. Does this challenge, which is based on the "theoretical plausibility criterion," provide a legitimate basis for physicians to discourage the use of these forms of CAM? The theoretical plausibility criterion asserts that (a) all valid knowledge will prove coherent with some characteristic of established contemporary science, and (b) the likelihood that a claim will eventually have this coherent relation to contemporary science can be judged on the basis of present knowledge *(24)*. Although some commentators object to the theory on the grounds that it may turn out false, even if it were true, it does not mean that we currently have enough information to judge which forms of CAM would be able to meet the test *(24)*.

The most obvious difficulty with the argument is that the failure of a CAM provider to provide a scientifically supportable biological mechanism for a given treatment modality does not, in itself, render the treatment unworthy of clinical consideration. It may merely point more to the limitation of our current state of scientific knowledge than a failure of the CAM modality in question.

Aspirin, for example, was first used as an analgesic more than 2500 years ago. The drug, derived from the white willow bark, was used effectively for centuries without a scientifically substantiated mechanism for action. In fact,

> today's scientists continue to be bewildered by just what aspirin's mechanisms of action are, discovering new modes of action, and how they relate to medical diagnostics. Whatever the science of aspirin, an intelligent person today takes it just as our ancestors did for millennia. Throughout time, explanations continue to vary just as purpose of administration does as well. Nevertheless, aspirin is perceived as being beneficial. *(25)*

As with the white willow bark, we may, in the future, discover a biological mechanism to explain how certain acupuncture points, or therapeutic touch, or massage therapy works on the body and mind. However, the lack of such an explanation does not, as some critics may suggest, provide grounds for discrediting those forms of CAM that lack a well-understood biological mechanism.

Despite the lack of a solid scientific foundation to explain the mechanism of action, there is growing evidence that some forms of CAM provide therapeutic benefits. Consider, for example, recent reports offering evidence of acupuncture as an effective adjunctive therapy for the treatment of osteoarthritis of the knee *(26)*. Even those critical of CAM acknowledge that a person does not have to accept the underlying theoretical framework for a particular CAM to recognize that clinical data may support its efficacy in treating some conditions *(21)*. Physicians may point out to their skeptical colleagues that the effectiveness of a particular CAM modality may actually point to the need for further study to identify the mechanism at work.

Physicians may also encounter colleagues who challenge some forms CAM because they, unlike conventional therapies, have not been demonstrated safe and effective by well-constructed studies. Although safety and efficacy are ethical concerns for physicians, this too is not limited to CAM. In "A Dose of Our Own Medicine: Alternative Medicine, Conventional Medicine, and the Standards of Science," the author considers this challenge and questions whether such concerns present an accurate picture of the difference between conventional and CAM practices *(27)*. Although it is true, she maintains, that many forms of CAM have not been subjected to rigorous scientific testing, the author suggests that the same arguments hold true for many forms of conventional medicine. It is now widely reported, although likely unknown to the average patient, that only a small percentage of conventional medicine has been subjected to the same rigorous standards of scientific scrutiny that some physicians claim is essential for CAM. In fact "the medical community has a long history of accepting new technologies, and new uses of existing technologies, with little science to connect theoretical foundations to such practical applications" *(27)*.

The major difficulty with the "lack of scientific evidence" argument is that it could be used to foster a double standard of evaluation. Here, the ethical concerns arise not from lowering the bar to allow CAM entry into conventional medicine, but from those physicians who may unfairly apply a double standard, raising the bar of evidence for CAM providers while applying a lower standard of evidence to justify their use of more conventional treatment.

What is troubling to proponents of CAM are physicians who apply "lack of scientific evidence" to discredit certain forms of CAM, yet fail to point out that physicians are often forced to engage in similar practices. They treat CAM unfairly only when they leave a patient with the impression that all conventional therapies have been thoroughly tested for safety and efficacy. This, however, misrepresents the current state of medical treatment. Although many therapies do in fact stem from such research initiatives, it is not true of all medical interventions.

Consider also a recent Associated Press story of a 15-year-old female diagnosed with what would usually be a fatal case of rabies *(28)*. According to the report, "lacking any other treatment, doctors gambled on the experimental [drug] combination and induced a coma to stave off the rabies infection." According to Rodney Willoughby, a pediatric disease infection specialist, "no one had really done this before, even in animals" *(28)*. In this case, physicians provided a therapeutic intervention for which there were no scientific studies to demonstrate either safety or efficacy. In fact, the treatment itself could have proven fatal. Yet, these physicians are praised because their gamble paid off.

Critics may challenge, however, that although there were no scientific studies to support the safety or efficacy of such a radical treatment for rabies, the hypothesis was at least based on sound scientific reasoning. Scientific methodologies offered a legitimate foundation on which to base their hypothesis and, at least in this case, it worked. Yet, although this may provide support for utilizing conventional therapies, it would not, as was suggested in the previous section, unilaterally discredit those forms of CAM that have not been subjected to such studies.

Radical treatment for rabies may be ethically justified in this case on the grounds that it offers some hope in fighting an otherwise fatal condition. More common, however, is the use of prescription drugs for "off-label" purposes. Physicians sometimes prescribe drugs for purposes, or for specific age groups, other than those for which the drug has been approved. One study found that nearly half of all prescriptions in a neonatal intensive care unit were used off label *(29)*. Another study found 10% of pediatric prescriptions were used off label in a general practice setting *(30)*. The authors of these studies caution that the practice remains widespread, with significant risks to patients.

Why would a physician use a drug for a purpose for which it has not been tested? It may be that a physician has had success with it in the past. There may not be an approved pharmaceutical to treat a specific condition, or for treatment within a certain age group, so the physician prescribes what he or she believes may work in this case. The difficulty with prescribing drugs off label is that it poses a significant risk of injury to a patient and may offer little, if any, benefit. Yet this is exactly the same problem that leads some physicians to criticize CAM.

This is not, however, to suggest that because physicians occasionally prescribe drugs that have not been proven safe and effective for the treatment of specific disorders that one should overlook the prescription practices of CAM providers. That is, the fact that physicians must sometimes resort to unproven therapies does not legitimize the use of every unproven therapy. What it does suggest is that CAM and conventional medicine are sometimes limited by insufficient studies to support certain treatment practices. To remedy this deficiency, both physicians and CAM providers have an ethical obligation to become actively engaged in research to ensure the quality, and accuracy, of their health care recommendations. Physicians should encourage their skeptical colleagues to acknowledge their obligation to encourage and support further research into CAM, not merely to dismiss it as unworthy of study because it fails to fit into the currently accepted medical paradigm.

Physicians must also be careful not to misrepresent their concerns with the safety of CAM. Undoubtedly, some forms of CAM may be quite dangerous. But, so are some forms of conventional medicine. The fact that a given conventional pharmaceutical was approved for use following randomized clinical trials does not, in itself, appear to guarantee its safety. Conventional drugs are sometimes pulled from the market once longitudinal studies demonstrate harmful side effects that were not recognized during initial testing. Recent controversies surrounding the drugs used for arthritis, hormone replacement therapies, and certain antidepressants for children are good examples. In many cases, the safety of conventional drugs is determined in much the same way that CAM providers determine efficacy of their treatments, through long-term observation of patient use. Accordingly, responsible physicians and CAM providers should subject their therapies to long-term studies.

The most common objections to CAM fail to hold up under further investigation. Not only do they fail to cast a shadow of doubt over the entire realm of untested CAM therapies, in many cases the objections against CAM apply equally to a variety of conventional treatment options. If restrictions were applied equitably, physicians would lose a wide range of conventional treatment modalities. Physicians need to take care when considering the difference between CAM and conventional treatment modalities. The potential integration of CAM affords physicians an opportunity to reflect on the differences that distinguish their care from that of CAM providers. Physicians have an ethical duty to treat CAM fairly. They must avoid exaggerating differences between conventional medicine and CAM. Physicians have a duty to take care in their assessment of CAM and engage in a dialogue that can better help their patients more effectively evaluate specific CAM treatment modalities.

DO PHYSICIANS HAVE A DUTY
TO INTEGRATE CAM
INTO CONVENTIONAL CARE?

Why integration? Although there are compelling ethical arguments supporting a physician's obligation to learn about CAM and to treat it fairly, why should physicians be concerned to integrate CAM into patient care? Some physicians undoubtedly see the recent surge of interest in examining CAM as an attempt, primarily by CAM providers, to legitimize treatment modalities that are currently marginalized in mainstream medicine. Yet patients themselves drive much of the current integration, as they, by their own choice, often utilize CAM alongside conventional treatment. This may be frustrating to those physicians who have long believed that advances in science and public education would lead to the decline and eventual eradication of nonconventional health systems. This hypothesis has proven to be untrue.

CAM is growing in popularity. CAM usage transcends the boundaries of race, ethnicity, religion, and social class, with certain forms of CAM being used almost exclusively by formally educated, middle-class groups *(8)*. The popularity of CAM has even encouraged some health insurance plans to provide coverage for CAM in order to attract customers, further motivating the trend toward integration. In essence, CAM is being integrated with or without the consent, or approval, of physicians.

The integration of CAM into conventional medicine raises a different set of ethical concerns for health care professionals. Thus far, my discussion of CAM has treated it as something outside of conventional medicine. Although one may argue that physicians have a duty to learn about CAM and to treat it fairly, recent literature suggests a new way of thinking about the relationship between CAM and conventional medicine. Some proponents of CAM suggests that the idea behind the shift to integrative medicine "is that eventually a single health system would include all of the treatment modalities currently encompassed by CAM and scientific medicine. The integrated system would still be based in science, but would extend beyond it" *(31)*.

This system would incorporate only those CAM modalities that have been shown to offer safe and effective treatment option. Here, the focus is on the method itself, not the underlying theory that may very well conflict with accepted scientific standards and theories. Although the biological mechanism may be unknown, the CAM modality can be incorporated so long as safety and efficacy have been sufficiently demonstrated.

Examples of such integration might include physicians who refer patients to chiropractors for the treatment of chronic back pain. Other examples could include referrals to acupuncturists for the treatment of chronic arthritis pain or referrals to a massage therapist. The ethical obligation to include these CAM modalities arises in several ways.

First, it may be something that the patient wants to try, or is currently using. Respecting the patient's autonomy here becomes important. It may also be obligatory in order to promote the patient's well-being and to prevent causing harm. A physician may find that a patient complaining of chronic pain could benefit from some forms of CAM, especially when there may be significant side effects associated with the recommended pharmaceutical. If a patient complaining of chronic pain reports benefits with CAM, especially if it limits or makes pharmaceutical interventions unnecessary, then the physician should encourage the patient to continue with that modality. In this way, physicians integrate CAM into conventional medicine.

In an integrative system, physicians may also have an obligation to provide patients with information about nonconventional treatment options. In some cases, a physician's ethical obligation to obtain informed consent may make the integration of certain CAM therapies necessary, especially when tests have been done that demonstrate their efficacy *(32)*. A patient suffering from mild yet uncomfortable pain in a joint may very well benefit from the services of a chiropractor, massage therapist, or acupuncturist. A physician may reasonably look to these alternatives to offer a first line of treatment for such conditions mentioned previously. In this way, the physician helps to promote the patient's well-being and minimizes the risk of potential harm.

In cases where there is insufficient evidence as to the safety and efficacy of a given form of CAM, and where professional standards for licensing and credentialing are not in place, physicians may nevertheless have some obligation to at least tolerate a patient's utilization of CAM. In these cases, the physician may not only reject the underlying theoretical justification for the CAM modality in question, but may find that the evidence supporting the efficacy of the modality weak enough to negate the obligation to inform a patient that the modality exists. Homeopathic remedies, spiritualists, or therapeutic touch offer a few examples. With these alternatives, it is generally efficacy, not safety, which is at issue. Although a physician is not obligated to refer a patient to a spiritualist, respect for patient autonomy creates a duty to tolerate such practices if the patient wishes to incorporate them into clinical care.

Patients may also wish to include CAM modalities when they offer treatments for conditions that are not recognized by, or may seem bizarre to, conventional providers. One example may be soul loss, a cross-culturally recognized spiritual condition that requires the prompt attention of a spiritual healer, but may also include symptoms and illness that may benefit from conventional treatment *(8)*. In order to maintain respect for the individual's cultural practices and value system, physicians should, even if they reject the theoretical foundations for a condition like soul loss, respect the patients view and work to incorporate CAM into the patient's care. Here, the ethical challenge that arises is one of providing medically responsible counseling while acknowledging and respecting the patient's values and beliefs *(32)*. Here, it may become necessary to coordinate efforts with the CAM provider and ensure that the treatment modalities recommended can be utilized safely along with conventional treatment.

Yet in demanding that physicians show respect for patient wishes, it is equally important that patients show respect for their health care professionals' values and beliefs. In some cases, it may not be possible to respect the patient's wishes and allow for the utilization of certain forms of CAM. A hospitalized patient, for example, may be reasonably restricted from certain spiritual or ritual practices that may create health risks or an unpleasant environment for other patients and employees. Although these are legitimate concerns, physicians should be cautious not to use this merely as a means of restricting practices that can otherwise be accommodated in clinical care.

Physicians have an ethical obligation to work toward the integration of CAM into conventional care. In some instances, the obligation stems from the need to provide a patient with the safest, least invasive, and most effective treatment available. When safe and effective alternatives to conventional therapies exist, physicians should be willing, and able, to explore these with their patients. Patients may also initiate integration. When a patient utilizes CAM modalities, whether because of personal desire or cultural and religious beliefs, physicians should be willing to assist the patient to achieve integration or refer the patient to another physician for information and/or care. The physician should not abandon the patient because of CAM use or interest. Here again, the commonly shared values of beneficence and autonomy help to establish the physician's ethical obligations in integrated medicine.

CONCLUSION

The rise in popularity of CAM continues to challenge physicians who must wrestle with the practical and ethical implications of integrated health care. Current research is beginning to show that certain forms of CAM offer safe and effective alternatives to conventional drugs and treatments. In order to promote and protect the health and well-being of their patients, physicians must develop an understanding of CAM and, in some situations, seek to incorporate CAM into conventional therapy.

In many cases, CAM offers more than an alternative to conventional medicine. In addition, it brings worldviews and values that may conflict with those of conventional medicine. Here, it is essential that physicians be able to embrace an ethical framework that allows them to incorporate a wide range of values. Although each patient encounter is likely to raise its own unique set of values and ethical concerns, certain ethical principles are now well established and provide a valuable tool for determining a physician's ethical obligations when dealing with CAM.

Physicians have an ethical obligation to learn about CAM, and to inquire about their patients' use of CAM. This is necessary both to protect the patient from possible harms and to promote the patient's well-being by providing the patient with enough information to make meaningful decisions about CAM. Physicians who systematically avoid CAM will be ill-prepared to fulfill these ethical obligations. In addition, physicians should treat CAM, and CAM providers fairly, and should not hold CAM to standards that conventional medicine is itself unable to achieve. Finally, physicians should strive to incorporate safe and effective forms of CAM into clinical care and either seek to accommodate patients who wish to utilize CAM alongside conventional medicine or refer them to other physicians when they cannot.

REFERENCES

1. Barnes P, Powell-Griner E, McFann K, Nahin R. CDC Advance Data Report no. 343. Complementary and alternative medicine use among adults: United States, 2002. May 27, 2004. Report available online at: http://nccam.nih.gov/news/report.pdf

1a. Eisenberg DM, Kessler RC, Foster C, et al. Unconventional medicines in the United States. Prevalance, cost and patterns of use. N Engl J Med 1993;328:246–252.

1b. Center for Medicare and Medicaid Services. 1997 National Survey Expenditures Survey available at www.cms.hhs.gov/statistics/nhe.

2. Brody H, Rygwelski, JM, Fetters, MD. Ethics at the interface of conventional and complementary medicine. In: Jonas W and Levin J, ed. Essentials of complementary and alternative medicine. Philadelphia: Lippincott Williams and Wilkins, 1999, pp. 46–56.

3. Sugarman J, Burk L. Physicians' ethical obligations regarding alternative medicine. JAMA 1998;280(18):1623–1625.

4. Nash R. The biomedical ethics of alternative, complementary, and integrative medicine. Altern Ther Health Med 1999;5(5):92–95.

5. Guinn D. Ethics and integrative medicine: moving beyond the biomedical model. Altern Ther Health Med 2001;7(6):68–72.

6. Cohen, M. Future medicine. Ann Arbor: The University of Michigan Press, 2003.

7. Cohen, M. Beyond complementary medicine: legal and ethical perspectives on healthcare and human evolution. Ann Arbor: The University of Michigan Press, 2000.

8. O'Connor, BB. Healing traditions: alternative medicine and the health professions. Philadelphia: University of Pennsylvania Press, 1995.

9. American Chiropractic Association website. Accessed: March 28, 2005. http://www.acatoday.com/content_css.ctm?CID=7/9

10. American Association of Naturopathic Physicians web site. Accessed: March 28, 2005. http://www.naturopathic.org/news/positions/ethics.aspx.

11. Beauchamp T, Childress J. Principles of biomedical ethics, 5th ed. New York: Oxford University Press, 2001.

12. Drisko J. Educating physicians about complementary and alternative medicine: increased understanding fosters improved communication. Clin Pract Altern Med 2001;2(3):189–193.

13. Kerridge I, McPhee J. Ethical and legal issues at the interface of complementary and conventional medicine. Med J Aust 2004; 181(3):164–166.

14. Barrett B. Alternative, complementary, and conventional medicine: is integration upon us? J Altern Complement Med 2003;9(3):417–427.
15. Williamson EM. Drug interactions between herbal and prescription medications. *Drug Safety* 2003;26(15):1075–1092.
16. Eisenberg D, Kessler R, Van Rompay MI, et al. Perceptions about complementary therapies relative to conventional therapies among adults who use both: results from a national survey. Ann Intern Med 2001;135:344–351.
17. Keenan P. Benefits of massage therapy and use of a doula during labor and childbirth. Altern Ther Health Med 2000;6(1):66–74.
18. Gilliland AL. Beyond holding hands: the modern role of the professional doula. JOGN Nurs 2002;31(6):762–769.
19. American Medical Association. Code of Medical Ethics. Chicago: Author, 2000.
20. American College of Physicians Ethics Manual, fifth edition. Ann Intern Med 2005;142:560–582.
21. Schneiderman L. Alternative medicine or alternatives to medicine? A physician's perspective. Camb Q Healthc Ethics 2000;9:83–97.
22. Barrett S. "Alternative" medicine: more hype than hope. In Humber J and Almeder R. eds. Alternative medicine and ethics. Totowa, NJ: Humana Press, 1998.
23. Angell M, Kassirer J. Alternative medicine—the risks of untested and unregulated remedies. N Engl J Med 1998;339(12):839–841.
24. Huffford D. Evaluating complementary and alternative medicine: the limits of science and of scientists. J Law Med Ethics 2003;31(2):198–212.
25. Riddle JM, History as a tool in identifying "new" old drugs. Adv Exp Med Biol 2002;505:89–94.
26. Berman, BM, Lao, L, Langenberg, P, Lee, WL, Gilpin, AMK, Hochberg, MC. Effectiveness of acupuncture as adjunctive therapy in osteoarthritis of the knee: a randomized, controlled trial. Ann Intern Med 2004;141(12):901–910.
27. Morreim EH. A dose of our own medicine: alternative medicine, conventional medicine, and the standards of science. J Law Med Ethics 2003;31(2):222–235.

28. Associated Press. Rabies treatment saves girl. Kansas City Star, November 24, 2004, sec. A6, p. 3.

29. O'Donnell CP, Stone RJ, Morley CJ. Unlicensed and off-label drug use in an Australian neonatal intensive care unit. Pediatrics 2002;110(5):e52.

30. McIntyre, J. Conroy S. Avery A. Corns H. Choonara I. Unlicensed and off label prescribing of drugs in general practice. Arch Dis Child 2000;83(6):498–501.

31. Sade R. Complementary and alternative medicine: foundations, ethics, and law. J Law Med Ethics 2003;31(2):183–190.

32. Adams K, Cohen M, Eisenberg D, Jonsen A. Ethical considerations of complementary and alternative medical therapies in conventional medical settings. Ann Intern Med 2002;137(8): 660–664.

4

Advising Patients and Communicating About Complementary and Alternative Medicine

Arti Prasad, MD
and Mariebeth B. Velásquez, BS

The art of communication is the language of leadership.

—*James Humes (1)*

INTRODUCTION

Complementary and alternative medicine (CAM) is a broad domain of resources that encompasses health systems, modalities, and practices and their accompanying theories and beliefs, other than those intrinsic to the dominant health system of a particular society or culture in a given historical period *(2)*. Other terms sometimes used to describe these health care practices include *natural medicine, nonconventional medicine,* and *holistic medicine*

From: *Biomedical Ethics Reviews: Complementary and Alternative Medicine: Ethics, the Patient, and the Physician*
Edited by: L. Snyder © Humana Press Inc., Totowa, NJ

(3). The widespread use of CAM therapies has been steadily increasing over the past few decades, yet there are few clear guidelines on how physicians should be advising patients about their use.

Epidemiological studies have shown that the lifetime prevalence of CAM use in the United States has increased steadily since the 1950s *(4)*. In a national survey published in 1993, one in three respondents (34%) reported using at least one form of CAM therapy in the previous year *(5)*. A Centers for Disease Control survey published in 2004 demonstrated that 36% of US adults, aged 18 years and older, used some form of CAM in the previous 12 months *(6)*. In a study conducted in New Mexico in people with arthritis, 90.2% of the 612 participants reported using CAM to treat their condition *(7)*.

Several reasons have been identified as to why patients visit CAM practitioners, and they are discussed in detail in Chapter 1. They include having a new or long-term health problem, shopping for health and wellness, feeling dissatisfied with conventional treatment, and believing in the general approach of CAM *(8)*. Along with being more educated and reporting poorer health status, the majority of patients use alternative medicine not as much as a result of being dissatisfied with conventional medicine, but largely because they find these health care alternatives to be more congruent with their own values, beliefs, and philosophical orientation toward health and life *(9)*.

With the increasing use of CAM, reports of adverse reactions have more than doubled in 3 years *(6)*. With the potential risk of adverse drug reactions or interactions, it is in the patient's best interest to inform their physicians of their CAM use. However, it has been noted that 70% of patients do not reveal their herbal use to their allopathic practitioners *(10)*. There are several possible reasons for this. Some have hypothesized a perceived polarization of attitudes between patients and physicians about the use of CAM and its effectiveness. Whatever the basis of nondisclosure, the sad fact is that patients are at risk of adverse events and substandard care if there is no patient–physician dialogue about CAM *(11,12)*.

On a separate note, even if patients were to disclose their use of CAM, the question of whether or not the physician feels well trained or educated on these topics still stands. In 1994, Borkan et al. demonstrated that physicians who use CAM for themselves or their families had a higher rate of patient referrals for CAM therapy *(13)*. Without a formalized curriculum in medical education specializing in CAM, physicians must resort to their own resources and information-finding efforts in order to support such a dialogue with patients (*see* Chapter 4). An unpublished survey (Agosta, Prasad, Shelley, July 2002 – March 2005) of primary care physicians (PCPs), conducted at the University of New Mexico clearly demonstrated that PCPs felt that information regarding massage, acupuncture, and stress reduction might be usefully included in the undergraduate medical curriculum. In addition, they also felt that familiarity with CAM contributes significantly to patient satisfaction. Incorporation of information regarding CAM into the undergraduate curriculum may be a means of increasing physician familiarity with CAM and integrative medicine.

The National Center for Complementary and Alternative Medicine (NCCAM) at the National Institutes of Health (NIH) has recently issued its second 5-year strategic plan, which seeks to "enhance understanding of the social, cultural, and economic factors relating to the use of CAM" *(14)*. Legal issues in the clinical setting revolve around credentialing and licensure of CAM practitioners, and the implications for physicians who advise patients about CAM therapies *(12)*. There are also many relevant ethical implications in designing research trials in integrative medicine *(15)*. Social issues include the persistent lack of communication between patients and providers concerning CAM and integrative medicine, which might lead to adverse herb–drug interactions *(11)*.

The Institute of Medicine's (IOM) recent report on CAM in the United States also calls for more attention and scholarly effort in ethical, legal, and social issues surrounding CAM and integrative medicine. The IOM executive summary recommends that schools of medicine "incorporate sufficient information about CAM into the standard curriculum... to enable licensed professionals to competently advise their patients on CAM" *(2)*.

With more people turning to CAM for disease prevention, treatment, and health promotion, there is a mounting need for scientific research to investigate the safety profiles of popular treatment modalities, establish clinical efficacy for selected indications, and develop proper educational and training modules for clinicians with patients using CAM. An important area that is lacking focus is an inclusive guide for physicians, CAM practitioners, and patients regarding advice and communication pertaining to CAM use. Such a guide should be based on a foundational approach and understanding of CAM, its impact and role in our health care system, and the manner in which dialogue should be introduced and maintained in the patient–physician relationship.

In this chapter, we take a comprehensive look at the "interconnectivity of patient, physician, and the CAM practitioner," identify certain key challenges faced by the three vertices of this triad, and suggest some strategies to overcome these challenges. The main purpose of this chapter is to provide an expansive guide for use by the active participants of any health care delivery mode. This guide will not only inform physicians, but also patients and CAM practitioners.

CHALLENGES FACED BY PHYSICIANS

In this era of information overload, practicing physicians face multiple challenges when communicating with patients about CAM. They must inquire about a patient's use of these

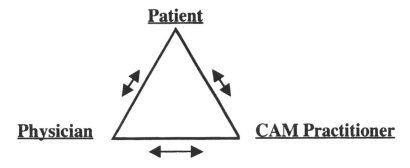

Fig. 1. The triad of interconnectivity.

therapies as some of them may be adjunctive, some may be useless, and some may be harmful or contraindicated for a patient's condition. These therapies may also carry the risk of adverse interactions with ongoing conventional medical treatments. Some patients may rely on these therapies to an extent that it might delay their acceptance of a proven therapy. The following discusses challenges that a practicing physician might face when his or her patients usc CAM therapies.

Knowledge

One learns peoples through the heart, not the eyes or the intellect.

—Mark Twain (16)

A physician can never know it all! A typical Western physician is neither trained nor experienced in the concepts and practice of CAM. Although the training of future physicians is gradually incorporating CAM cducation, there is no standardized curriculum in CAM *(17)*. Physicians who have had culturally diverse experiences may have a better understanding of this subject. However, as a culturally diverse physician, the first author has frequently experienced in her own career that training in the Western biomedical model is so dominant that it often over-

Table 1
Areas of Knowledge Limitation for Physicians

1. Various CAM modalities including taditional systems of medicine
2. Natural health care products: their safety, efficacy, interactions with herbs, drugs, and food
3. NCCAM's 5-year strategic plan and latest research in CAM
4. State and federal guidelines on the regulation of CAM practices, practitioners, and products
5. Local and federal guidelines on credentialing and licensure of CAM practitioners
6. Reliable databases, websites, books, journals, and other resources on CAM

whelms the experiences, values, and beliefs of other cultures. In addition, physicians might be so involved in their own area that they may not have much information on the advancements in other fields such as CAM. Few physicians are familiar with the latest CAM research, practice guidelines, legal and ethical issues, natural health care products (NHP), CAM credentialing and licensure, and reliable sources of information about CAM. (*See* Table 1 for areas of knowledge limitations for physicians.)

Attitudes

A strong positive mental attitude will create more miracles than any wonder drug.

—Patricia Neal (16)

As previously discussed, knowledge of and familiarity with CAM is only one component of the bigger picture. A solid knowledge base by itself is not enough, for a physician must also successfully bridge the communication gap between patients, CAM providers, and themselves. Perlman et al. assert that physicians discourage open discussion of CAM because of their lack of knowledge and desire not to appear uninformed *(18)*. Additionally, physicians have a difference of opinion about accepting, suggesting, or supporting CAM. Some may be skeptical of change when it involves unfamiliar territory. Some physicians may have had negative personal experiences with CAM or have had observed harm in a patient using CAM. It is difficult, if not impossible to change these attitudes. However, in the interest of best serving the patient, it is imperative that physicians consider including CAM therapies in the treatment plan if the patient expresses such a desire and if the therapy is proven to be generally safe.

Communication Skills

Effective questioning brings insight, which fuels curiosity, which cultivates wisdom.

—Chip Bell (19)

Physician communication skills vary, and we know that this can be a barrier to an effective patient–physician relationship. They must work at acquiring tools for analyzing communication with patients in order to assume partnership in understanding disease and establishing a collaborative, team approach to treatment. It has been documented that the embodiment of patient-centeredness and the biopsychosocial approach to the interview process is more conducive to effective communication, as well as a more recent emphasis on relationship-centered care *(20)*.

Many topics are difficult for the patient or the physician to broach, and patients are not likely to raise a topic if they feel judged or anticipate a negative reaction. If a physician—as a "professional expert"—can introduce and discuss the topic of CAM in a nonjudgmental way, the patient might feel less vulnerable and be more candid. An open-minded physician is more likely to elicit an open and honest response from a patient. If the physician judges the patient's story and content negatively, the patient is unlikely to share anything else with the physician *(21)*. Being open to discussion as well as more casual and friendly about CAM therapies will not only build trust between the two parties, but may also enhance adherence to treatment plans.

Fear of Endorsement

Advice is like snow—the softer it falls, the longer it dwells upon, and the deeper in sinks into the mind.

—Samuel Taylor Coleridge (1)

The past 20 years of keen interest in CAM have generated vigorous debates and ethical concerns (the ethical implications of advising patients on CAM are discussed in Chapter 2). One authoritative view is that "complementary therapies require an even greater appreciation of ethical concerns (than conventional medicine), given the nonmeasurable, nonrational dimensions of holistic practice." This is particularly the case "in therapies which do have a highly technical skill base, where ethical, rather than therapeutic, complaints are likely to give greater cause for concern" *(22)*. The differences in training and practice between conventional physicians and CAM practitioners also contribute toward the apprehension of physicians when it comes to recommending CAM. Without a complete understanding of CAM, there is a natural tendency for physicians to resist recommending CAM for the fear of jeopardizing the reputation of their own practice. In our interactions with colleagues, examples of this fear have been played out at all levels, including medical student organizations, professional societies, and private practices.

Lack of Cultural Competency

Culture is the arts elevated to a set of beliefs.

— Thomas Wolfe (1)

Competence, like truth, beauty and contact lenses, is in the eye of the beholder.

—Laurence J. Peter (16)

Differences in cultural and personal values contribute to challenges and barriers bctwccn physicians and patients. As the use of CAM permeates our society, the goal of relationship-centered care can be harmed by the absence of a respectful and sensitive attempt to communicate across cultural medical barriers *(18)*. In Hawaii, where there is a diverse ethnic population, physicians favor CAM training, have positive attitudes about CAM, and practice CAM therapies *(23)*. The medical profession should serve as a resource of information and skills that can be incorporated in an integrative manner with the appropriate complementary regimens that resonate with the cultural and individualist needs of each patient *(24)*. Physicians need not have a full understanding of every different culture but rathcr, adopt the practice of cultural humility by developing respectful attitudes towards different points of view as well as self-awareness of one's own beliefs.

Time Constraints

We must use time as a tool, not as a crutch.

—John F. Kennedy (16)

Patients, who are proponents of CAM and are current users, may have a wealth of knowledge about particular CAM therapies—often more than the physicians. They may not be well versed in the recent scientific literature on CAM, nor are they interested in learning about it. Their ultimate goal may only be "to get well." Patients have often read magazines; browsed the Internet multiple times; and have talked to friends and family before coming to the office with stacks of printed material for the physician to peruse. Do physicians have time to go through this material and also talk and listen to the patient during visits in the current health care environment? The answer is probably not.

The average HMO physician spends about 7 minutes with each patient, hardly conducive to lengthy patient–doctor communication and holistic therapy. Meanwhile, the average CAM practitioner spends 30 minutes with each patient *(25)*. Patients value CAM providers for providing emotional support and for listening *(26)*. Frenkel et al. and Adler et al. reported that patients did not raise issues about CAM because they believed that their disclosure of CAM use was not relevant or would not yield any benefit to the conventional treatment received, and that their physicians were unable or unwilling to contribute useful information about their CAM use *(27,28)*.

PHYSICIAN RESPONSIBILITIES

The identification of the barriers is only half the battle. What can be done to alleviate the separation between conventional and CAM treatment once the barriers are identified? Physicians must play an integral part in bridging the gap between the two different worlds of conventional medicine and CAM. They are responsible for establishing a welcoming environment, open communication, assessing the safety and effectiveness of a therapy, information gathering, and additional special considerations. If these responsibilities are fulfilled, then patients are well on their way toward integrative care, centered on their own needs and desires.

CAM has always been around but in the last decade it has gathered enough momentum to be seen as a "disruptive innovation" that is here to stay. Physicians need to learn more about the subject, its scope and limitations, and its safety and efficacy, as they strive to assist their patients in making informed and educated decisions. A physician need not be an expert in this area, but should have enough knowledge and interest to guide his or her patients, and be able to refer them to skilled CAM practitioners as appropriate. Such an approach is very much in line with the true meaning of the Latin word "doctor" namely, "teacher."

Create a Welcoming Environment

In order to open the dialogue about CAM between patients and physicians, an open-minded, unassuming, and welcoming environment must first be established. Mackenzie et al. remind us that a physician's nonverbal communication is observed by the patient in order to assess the physician's degree of respect, judgment, and compassion (29). For example, lack of eye contact by the caregiver is perceived as disapproval or lack of interest. Perlman et al. recommend that CAM be raised as a topic, and that it be raised by conveying a supportive attitude, along with the ability to listen for "nonverbal cues," encouraging further disclosure and discussion in response (18). Discussions of CAM should be approached in the same way as any sensitive topic about which patients may fear disapproval. Adler et al. found that patients are not looking for the physician's belief in or endorsement of CAM therapies, but appreciate those who were respectful, open-minded, willing to listen, and honest about the limitations of their own knowledge of CAM (28). Given the vast base of information available regarding CAM, the physician is unlikely to know everything about all CAM therapies. However, an attitude and approach of humility on the part of the physician seems to be effective and appreciated by patients seeking holistic treatment.

The process of patient reassurance starts from the time a physician walks into an exam room. The way in which the physician greets, looks, and talks to the patient all have an immediate effect on the patient's trust and respect for the physician. Creating a welcoming environment by means of openness; asking nonjudgmental questions about the use of drugs, herbs, and supplements; and discussing patients' approaches for prevention and wellness together provide a venue for further discussion of CAM.

Open Communication

> The most basic of all human needs is the need to understand
> and be understood. The best way to understand people is to
> listen to them.

—Ralph Nichols (19)

The basic building block of good communication is the feeling that every human being is unique and possesses values. Communication also includes active "listening." A caring physician should give complete attention to a patient discussing CAM without interruption, and with encouraging nonverbal cues. The patient must feel respected, heard, and appreciated. The physician may or may not agree with the patient but may want to take this time as a learning opportunity, and to just be with that person. Physicians may be delighted to see the results of such an encounter, in both the relationship with the patient, the healing response, and their own professional satisfaction. With the advances in the field of medicine over the last 30 years, there has been more emphasis on problem-driven approaches rather than that of healing. The concept of healing focuses on the return to wellness, rather than on the complexities of the problem. Physicians used to have the reputation of being "healers," but are no longer perceived as such because of their focus on "sickness" or "illness" vs "wellness." The "new healers," who are not physicians but CAM practitioners, have emerged and patients have reported more satisfaction with them because of their willingness and ability to listen, coupled with their open dialogue of values centered on wellness.

The skill and ability to listen also teaches physicians to learn patience. They must wait for their turn to talk and can interject only after they have given their full attention to the patient's story. It is important to determine why patients desire a particular therapy. Is it because their friend benefited from it or perhaps they saw an advertisement in a magazine or testimonials on the web? The underlying reasons behind patients' motivations are windows into how patients view their health and health care. Once this concept is accepted, a wider corridor to communication will be exposed.

Show Empathy

> When dealing with people, remember you are not dealing with creatures of logic, but creatures of emotion.
>
> —*Dale Carnegie (1)*

Empathy is a specific issue that needs special mention. Empathy is different from sympathy, which is generally viewed, as "I would like to help you." Empathy on the other hand, is a physician's ability to enter a patient's inner world, to "feel" the patient's pain and concerns (30). In a patient–physician encounter, a physician needs to demonstrate both curiosity and objectivity. Even if the patient's beliefs do not concur with the physician's own values and beliefs, the physician should remember that these may hold a huge psychological value for the patient. A patient's discussion of CAM with a physician reflects the patient's inner thinking, values, and beliefs. A physician needs to determine if this particular therapy is in agreement with the patient's particular cultural beliefs and personal values. In practice, the first author always finds it very rewarding and helpful to show curiosity by asking how people in their own culture would take care of a sick person. Patients have generally shown appreciation for the display of genuine interest and have found this gesture a rewarding experience.

Set Realistic Goals

The decision to support or recommend CAM is an important one. These are some of the topics to be considered before recommending a therapy: the therapy's safety and effectiveness, the expertise and qualifications of the CAM practitioner, the quality of the service delivery, and the assessment of risk–benefit ratio. The physician must ensure that conventional medical evaluation has been completed and standard options have been discussed and understood. The physician should assist patients in setting realistic goals for their CAM or integrative care. It can be challenging to work with patients who are looking and hoping to find a cure for their life threatening or chronic illness. The job of a physician is to bring the conversation to a common ground where there is understanding and respect for both the patient's and the physician's views and values. An example of an unrealistic goal would be to "find a cure for an incurable cancer" vs a realistic goal of "finding comfort and quality of life at the end of life."

Obtain More Information and Follow Up

With respect to training and education in CAM, physicians must familiarize themselves with reliable resources in order to assist patients with their treatment choices. Physicians should be familiar with important databases such as the Cochrane Collaboration database and the Natural Medicine Comprehensive Database and consult them when looking for current clinical evidence on CAM *(25)*. Studies have shown that physician knowledge, training, and experience using CAM were positively correlated with the physicians' attitudes toward and practice referral patterns with CAM *(13,23,31)*. Until formalized CAM educational programs are implemented into medical school curricula, only a familiarization with dependable CAM resources can provide the basic foundation of knowledge for physicians.

Having open communications, demonstrating curiosity, and accepting a lack of understanding but willingness to learn about the cultural and CAM practices of patients give physicians an opportunity to explore and advance their knowledge. As life-long learners, physicians can only benefit from a databank that grows bigger and broader with new information that can be used to help other patients. Showing their willingness to research the subject and getting back to patients at their next visit buys physicians

Table 2
Decision-Making Grid

Modalities that should be recommended	Modalities that should be accepted	Modalities that should be discouraged
Evidence supports efficacy	Evidence regarding is inconclusive	Evidence indicates inefficacy
And	**But**	**Or**
Evidence supports safety	Evidence supports safety	Evidence indicates serious risk

time, improves patient confidence in them, and encourages the patient to return. As a physician, one may want to use this as an opportunity for self-reflection and learning about something new and refreshing. Noting that self-reflection doesn't come easily to everyone, John Crellin and Fernando Ania, in their book *Professionalism and Ethics in Complementary and Alternative Medicine*, very eloquently described various suggestions on how to foster this, that rest on asking questions about oneself and the situation one is in *(30)*.

If physicians find reliable information on the CAM subject area, they should assess the quality of the study, and then the safety and effectiveness of the therapy. Generally, a safe product or practice is one that does no harm when used under defined conditions and as intended. Effectiveness is the likelihood of benefit from a practice, treatment, or technology applied under typical conditions by the average practitioner for the typical patient. Based on this information, physicians should use the guidelines for advising patients on sliding-scale evidence—the higher the toxicity and invasiveness of a therapy or a procedure, the higher the threshold for evidence for its effectiveness. We propose using the decision-making grid on acceptance, rejection, and discouragement of a particular CAM modality based on its safety and efficacy *(32; see* Table 2).

Physicians must develop a trusting relationship with patients to be able to openly discuss, evaluate, recommend, or refute a certain CAM therapy. They must also be open to referring the patient to another health care professional if the relationship and trust break down and they are not able to come to a common ground.

Provide Information on Reliable Resources

Physicians need to serve as a resource for patients to weigh the risks and benefits of any CAM therapy under consideration. When considering CAM therapy, it is important to consider what the patient's motivation is, whether he or she is looking for a cure, longer survival, improved quality of life, more control of health care, or something else *(33)*. It is the physician's duty to advise patients about potentially harmful aspects of CAM modalities, possible interactions, contraindications with synthetic medications, and current disease states *(34)*. It is the physician's professional obligation to monitor therapies with suspected or documented toxicity, and advise patients that an absence of documented toxicity for herbs, supplements, or chemical preparations does not equal safety *(12)*. By familiarizing themselves with the resources available to patients, physicians can facilitate and illuminate the path for the patient's self-motivated investigations.

In order to advise patients appropriately, it is necessary for physicians to have access to reliable information about CAM therapies. Relevant data include description of modalities, efficacy, a profile of risks and side effects, and common clinical indications treated by specific modalities. Many physicians acknowledge that they do not feel confident to discuss CAM with their patients due to a lack of training, and need further education in this field *(35)*. With the vast volumes of information pertaining to CAM currently available, it is unrealistic to expect conventional physicians to acquire a mastery of CAM education and knowledge. It may, in fact, be of greater value for physicians to adopt more effective approaches and communication styles that help to nurture the patient–physician relationship, support a patient-centered approach to treatment, and guide access to essential reliable resources for both patients and physicians. These resources can provide solid, credible evidence necessary for a careful evaluation of CAM treatment options and to inform and support recommendations to patients *(36)*.

The literature supports the evidence of a new trend toward formalized training and CAM education for physicians across the globe and in various stages of their careers. In July 2000, the Australian Medical Council released a position statement encouraging medical schools to devise teaching and learning strategies that address the understanding of CAM *(37)*. At Southampton University, an evaluation of a CAM module for third-year medical students demonstrated increased interest in CAM, increased confidence, and the development of holistic approaches to treating patients *(38)*. The University of Arizona offers a fellowship in CAM, focusing on integrative medicine described as a comprehensive system that has an evidence base and also addresses consumers' demands *(27)*. For physicians already established in a practice, there is evidence that continuing medical education courses on various CAM therapies remain well accepted and in great demand *(39,40)*.

Examine the Practitioner's Expertise

A responsible physician may want to investigate a particular CAM practitioner whom a patient desires to visit. We recommend talking to the CAM practitioner directly about his or her training and experience with a particular condition. An important piece of information is the CAM practitioner's credentialing and licensure *(33)*. The referring physician should know whether a CAM provider is licensed, certified, and insured and this information should be documented in the patient's chart. After identifying a suitable provider, the physician should obtain the patient's permission to release relevant information to the CAM provider in

order to offer accurate historical information and avoid conflicting recommendations *(12)*. Physicians' obligation is to find the
evidence, evaluate it, and make professional recommendations to
patients to the best of their knowledge. In this sense, CAM therapies are not very different from conventional therapies that are
routinely subjected to high scrutiny.

Assess the Costs

Another element of the information-gathering process is to
provide the patient with all of the data available, including a cost
analysis of the proposed CAM therapy. When considering costs,
it is important that the physicians assess what the patient is expect-
ing from CAM therapy, whether that is a realistic objective, and
then weigh the estimated costs with possible benefits and consequences. The potential for economic harm of the patient should
be well established before referring the patient to CAM therapy.
Kaegi *(33)* suggests that information should be gathered from
proponents and opponents or each CAM modality for consideration. If rigorous research shows that a particular CAM therapy
or procedure is safe and effective, physicians should help make it
accessible for responsible use.

Check the Delivery of Service

It is extremely important to assess patient safety when a physician refers a patient to a CAM practitioner. This is quite a legitimate concern in all medical encounters. Physicians must
remember that patients want referral for a more "holistic" or a
healing-based approach and so the ambiance of the CAM practitioners' office should be consistent with it. The patient may have
screened a CAM practitioner's office to look at the set up, schedules, follow-up process, etc., but as a physician in integrative
practice, the first author recommends a "field trip" and a "show
and tell" personal experience in that practitioner's office. Although
not routinely practiced by physicians to visit another conven-

tional medical specialist, they may opt to visit a CAM practitioner owing to the general unfamiliarity with CAM practices. This may not fit very well a busy physician's schedule, but we have observed that many CAM practitioners are happy to have a conventional physician come in for a visit or a treatment.

Monitor Progress

Assuming that a fruitful relationship has been established between the physician and the CAM practitioner, it is now the physician's responsibility to monitor progress. We have frequently noticed that once a patient is referred to a CAM practitioner, some physicians consider their responsibility to be over, but this is the beginning of a new responsibility. Physicians should encourage their patients to keep an open communication with them, make follow-up visits with them so they can monitor the effects of a therapy. This also gives them an opportunity to review the possibilities of herb–drug interactions in any synergistic treatment plan. Physicians should leverage this educational opportunity to hear about the CAM therapy itself and about the effectiveness of the integration first hand from the patients before going to the next step.

Change Attitude

Overtime, we all change in terms of our thinking and attitudes toward life. With effective relationships and transparent communication, we expect a paradigm shift in physician's attitude about CAM and its integration with modern medicine. Like many other integrative physicians, the first author in her own professional career, has witnessed this shift in the attitude of many generalists and specialists. The trend of health care should carry us toward patient-centered care, in an ideal sense. If we are to be true to this ideal, our training and foci should be patient- and data-driven, which would validate our need for the integration of CAM into conventional medicine. An increasing number of statistics from current studies are producing evidence that supports the assertions that patient use and demand for CAM is present and steadily increasing. It is our responsibility to remain present in that movement and our challenge to be proactive in its progress.

CHALLENGES FACED BY PATIENTS

The second vertex of the connectivity triad is patients. The flow of knowledge, the sharing of ideas and the awareness of cultural and personal values all should be facilitated during a patient–physician encounter. Our current environment supports and rewards only the physician in these encounters. In most situations, the dialogue is one-sided and the patient often feels unheard and as though he or she is not represented during such a meeting. The following section discusses challenges that patients may experience.

Knowledge

When you know a thing, to hold that you know it; and when you do not know a thing, to allow that you do not know it— this is knowledge.

—Confucius, the Confucian Analects (16)

It is important to stress that even sophisticated consumers have an overly optimistic view of CAM. It is perceived by many as "natural" medicine and thus safe. Patients are at a loss when it comes to accessing and comprehending the very latest research information on a specific health matter. A popular approach involves searching news media and the Internet to get information on CAM and integrative medicine.

The published data suggest that consumers underestimate the risk of side effects of CAM. Consumers have no idea how to report side effects when they occur. Patients may also be unclear as to how they should find a credentialed CAM practitioner and

Table 3
Areas of Knowledge Limitations for Patients

1. Various CAM modalities and ways to integrate them with Western medicine
2. Natural health care products: their safety, efficacy, interactions with herbs, drugs, and food
3. Latest research in CAM
4. State and federal guidelines on the regulation of CAM practices, practitioners, and products
5. State and federal guidelines on credentialing and licensure of CAM practitioners
6. Access to reliable databases, websites, books, journals, and other resources on CAM

where to turn if they have a complaint. The consumer can be uninformed, misinformed, or mislead by the media, by the labeling of NHP, by getting information through their network of family and friends, and through false advertisement of CAM practices and practitioners. (*See* Table 3 on areas of knowledge limitations for patients.)

Attitude

Change your thoughts and you change the world.

—*Norman Vincent Peale (1)*

A subset of patients who are predisposed to CAM may approach their physicians with a prejudice against conventional medicine. This bias may have stemmed from a negative experience or these patients might have witnessed a close family member's suffering during conventional medical treatment. There is also a belief that CAM is gentler, less toxic, and more natural. This negative attitude toward conventional medicine causes a huge obstacle for patient–physician communication. It is then extremely "natural" for the physician in turn to take a negative attitude toward CAM as a direct result of this encounter. Patients, too. must understand the necessity of mutual respect when interacting with physicians.

Patient nondisclosure of CAM use can largely be the result of personal convictions on the patient's part. The most frequently cited reason for lack of disclosure is the feeling that the physician was "not interested in the patient's use of CAM" *(28)*. The literature supports the assertion that most disclosure about the use of CAM only occurs when physicians directly ask their patients about such use *(26,41,42)*. In fact, clinicians will miss 80–90% of all CAM utilization if they do not directly inquire about such practices *(26)*. With such preconceived notions that physicians will frown on their use of CAM, patients, in withholding information about their CAM use, are contributing to the substantial barrier that prevents the focus of patient-centered care.

Communication Skills

> Asking the right questions takes as much skill as giving the right answers.
>
> *—Robert Half (1)*

Like some physicians who are not skilled in opening a communication channel, many patients lack this skill as well. They may have no idea about the consequences—whether poor or favorable—of sharing their use of CAM and establishing partnerships with their physicians. The first author sees many CAM practitioners as patients in her clinical practice. These "CAM" patients possess several qualities. Not only are they skilled practitioners, but they also are role models for self-care and wellness. They are also respectful of conventional medicine and are good communicators and integrators. On the other hand, many of her other patients do not possess the communication skills that are needed to build a positive relationship. Often, such patients are a challenge to physicians with what are seen as unrealistic demands and resistance to good advice. As previously discussed, when the patient–physician relationship lacks an open, nonjudgmental fluidity, both parties are prevented from achieving a high-quality health care experience.

Fear of Rejection

I think all great innovations are built on rejections.

—*Louise Nevelson (1)*

It is important to note that the patient is in a vulnerable position in a typical physician–patient encounter. Patients often visit their doctors in the hope of having a collaborative relationship to achieve optimum health, yet they are hesitant to disclose information about CAM use. They have a fear of rejection or losing this relationship if they were to ask questions about CAM. Even if they have read about or researched a particular therapeutic modality, they may feel embarrassed or ashamed to bring it up with a professional expert. As an internist practicing medicine for more than 15 years, it is the experience of the first author that patients understand their physical bodies, and have some sense of what is wrong with them and what they need to do to alleviate a particular problem. They are looking for an opportunity to share it with their physician and if the physician fails to elicit this information or deliberately ignores it, the patient loses trust in that particular physician's ability or desire to help.

Cultural and Personal Values

Culture is the name for what people are interested in, their thoughts, their models, the books they read and the speeches they hear, their table-talk, gossip, controversies, historical sense and scientific training, the values they appreciate . . .

—*Walter Lippmann (1)*

It must be remembered that each person has his or her own needs. The concepts of many CAM practices are very attractive to people because they are congruent with popular belief systems. For example, the need for balance in life, for spirituality, or to fulfill cultural needs are well aligned with some people's personal values. People want to seek greater personal control in health and illness whether for a life-threatening or chronic condition. They believe that an individual has responsibilities toward health maintenance and illness, and therefore they find it good practice to try out new health ideas, sometimes regardless of scientific evidence.

Access and Cost Issues

Access to a competent, credible, and reliable CAM therapist may look simple but in reality is quite challenging. The self-promotion tactics adopted by some CAM practitioners are misleading to consumers. Patients are subject to clever marketing strategies and whose product captures their eye and fits the true needs of their lifestyle, rather than more reliable means of assessing which therapies would be most beneficial to their health. Although many pay out of pocket for CAM services, the cost of these therapies can still be prohibitive for a majority of patients because, with the exception of some chiropractic and acupuncture benefits, health insurers do not cover them.. And even more people lack basic health insurance, which creates a direct link between these high costs, causing limited accessibility for patients.

PATIENT RESPONSIBILITIES

Physicians alone are not to blame when they are not able to provide information, advise patients, or assist them in making correct choices to achieve optimum health. Patients have an equal responsibility to be active participants in their health care. They should be well informed about their health so that they can become fully involved in their health care and perhaps even become their own "doctor," and physicians become their "coaches."

Be an Informed Consumer

The new generation of consumers is generally better informed and more confident than those of the past. As consumers of health care, and in particular of CAM, however, this assumption may not be true. Although much information is available, objective, and reliable information is less available. (*See* Chapter 5 on medical and patient education on CAM.) But the decision to use CAM is an important one. At a minimum, before selecting a CAM therapy ,patients should consider the following: the safety and effectiveness of the therapy or treatment, the expertise and qualifications of the health care practitioner, and the quality of the delivery of service *(43,44)*. These topics should be considered when selecting any practitioner or therapy and not just CAM.

Open Communications

Patients must remember that the best care results from the integration of the best of both worlds. Neither conventional medicine nor CAM has all the answers. It is in the patient's own best interest to volunteer his or her inclinations and ideas. Physicians may or may not be receptive to them based on their prior experience, personal and professional bias, and lack of education and training in this area. As a practicing physician, the first author appreciates the information that she receives from her patients and learns from it. If physicians do not have enough knowledge or interest in CAM, patients should feel free to ask for a referral to another physician who is more knowledgeable and would be willing to help. Patients may have a more successful outcome with another physician.

Discuss the Safety and Efficacy
of a Therapy

Many physicians feel that specific information on CAM safety and effectiveness may be less readily available than information about conventional medical treatments. Research on these therapies is ongoing and continues to grow but it is not difficult to find the information if their physician is willing to try. There are many reliable sources such as Medline, PubMed, Cochrane Database, and other online resources to which the major medical libraries are now subscribing. Patients should allow enough time for physicians to tap into these resources. On a follow-up visit, they should discuss the safety and efficacy of a particular therapy and make an informed decision based on this discussion. They may also want to have a similar discussion with their CAM provider particularly about the safety and effectiveness of a desired treatment. This discussion is an opportunity for them to share with both their physician and CAM practitioner about all alternative or conventional treatments and therapies that they may already be receiving, as this information must be folded into any consideration of the safety and effectiveness of the entire treatment plan.

Research the CAM Practitioner's Expertise
and Background

An informed patient may want to take a closer look into the background, qualifications, licensing, and competence of a CAM practitioner. The practice of CAM usually is not as well regulated as the practice of conventional medicine. Licensing, accreditation, and regulatory laws, however, are increasingly being implemented. Appropriate state licensing of education and practice is the only way to ensure that the practitioner is competent and can provide quality services. Most, but not all, types of CAM practices have national organizations of practitioners that are familiar with legislation, state licensing, certification, and registration laws.

Patients can contact a state or local regulatory agency with authority over practitioners who practice the therapy or treatment they seek. Local and state medical boards, other health regulatory boards or agencies, and consumer affairs departments provide information about a specific practitioner's license, education, and accreditation, and whether there are any complaints lodged against the practitioner. They should also check to see if the practitioner is licensed to deliver the services the practitioner says they deliver. Some organizations will direct consumers to the appropriate regulatory agencies in their state and these agencies can provide referrals and information about specific practitioners.

Talk to Other Health Consumers

Patients should consult with their friends and colleagues who have had experience with specific practitioners. They may wish to find out about the competence and reputation of the practitioner in question, and whether there have ever been any complaints from patients and other health care providers.

Talk to the CAM Practitioner

Finding a practitioner who is easily accessible is a complex task. Patients may wish to talk with several practitioners before choosing to work with one. A typical set of questions they might wish to ask the practitioner is outlined in Table 4. Their physician may provide a referral to a CAM practitioner if the physician has developed a working relationship with a particular CAM practitioner. Patients should feel comfortable asking questions about the practitioner's education, additional training, licenses, and certifications, both traditional and nontraditional. They should ask about the practitioner's approach to treating a particular problem. More importantly, they need to know how open the practitioner is when it comes to communication with their physician about treatment protocols, possible side effects, and potential problems. Patients may want to make sure that the CAM practitioner is will-

Table 4
What to Ask a CAM Practitioner

1. Is this particular therapy a recognized treatment for my disorder?
2. What is your educational and training background?
3. Can you share some research on the safety and efficacy of this treatment?
4. Do you have experience and success treating my symptoms or disorder?
5. How many patients have you successfully treated using this particular therapy?
6. What is the length and cost of the proposed treatment?
7. How long have you been practicing this therapy?
8. What are your other professional competencies?
9. What other kinds of problems do you treat?
10. How many patients do you see in a day?
11. How comfortable do you feel working in collaboration with my primary care physician?
12. How would you communicate with my physician?
13. How do you assess the effectiveness of this treatment?
14. What is the stopping point in the treatment protocol?
15. Are patient education or professional references available?

ing to consult with their physician if and when the treatment does not work. After selecting a practitioner, the education dialogue for integrative health care begins between the patient, physician, and CAM practitioner.

Assess the Costs

Costs are an important factor to consider because many CAM treatments are not currently reimbursed by health insurance. Many patients pay directly for these services. They should inquire with their CAM practitioner and health insurer as to which treatments and therapies are reimbursable. Sometimes employer's insurance company or state's free or discounted care program may cover or offer discounted health and wellness services such as chiropractic, yoga, or fitness classes. If problems are work related, the worker's comp program may allow for free or discounted therapies such as chiropractic or massage. Patients may wish to call, query their latest policies, and give them feedback if the services are not covered because many insurers are considering expanding their coverage to include CAM and would like to hear from consumers.

Some of the best therapists are costly, so patients should assess what they can truly afford and what all their options are for addressing their health goals. They should also determine the out-of-pocket expense for health and wellness vs other projected expenditures in their lives.

Consumers should conduct cost comparisons for a particular service in order to get a general idea. Regulatory agencies and professional associations also may provide cost information. They may want to negotiate a price with their practitioner. Certain CAM practitioners or health centers have sliding scales or may offer discounted services if financial hardships are explained. Some will offer a discount if patients commit to a series of treatments. It's also worth inquiring about the possibility of trading. Some CAM practitioners may agree to give free treatments in exchange for a service they need, such as home or office repair, child care, house cleaning, or handiwork. It is acknowledged that this bartering system is not typically practiced in conventional medicine. The ethical reason behind this difference is not clear.

Check the Delivery of the Service

Although quality of service is not necessarily related to the effectiveness or safety of a treatment or practice, it is important to consider under what conditions, and how the treatment or therapy is delivered. The primary issue to consider is whether the service delivery adheres to regulated standards for medical safety and care.

A welcoming and healing environment aids in the healing process and recovery. Patients should visit the practitioner's office or clinic and ask about the number of patients typically seen in a day or week, and how much time the practitioner spends with each patient. They should evaluate the conditions of the office or clinic. They should assess if the costs of the service is excessive for what is delivered.

Keep the Communication Open With Physicians

As vested consumers in their health care, patients should discuss all issues with their physician concerning treatment side effects, adverse effects, and additive effects. They should remember that CAM care is an opportunity for all three parties to gain education. Effective and productive health care management requires knowledge of both conventional and CAM therapies for the practitioner to have a complete picture of the treatment plan. Patients are paving the way for future health consumers seeking integrative health care.

CHALLENGES FACED BY CAM PRACTITIONERS

The triad of interconnectivity cannot be fully drawn without the CAM practitioners in the picture. They play an equally important role in facilitating the positive patient–physician–CAM practitioner relationship. It is an opportunity for them to share their knowledge and experience with the conventional physician and make them aware of the role they can play in improving the quality of health care of patients. They are in a position to give advice and guidance to patient and their physician. In our interactions with many CAM practitioners over a number of years, some common challenge themes have emerged.

Table 5
Areas of Knowledge Limitations for CAM Practitioners

1. Concepts of conventional medicine and ways to integrate them with CAM
2. Natural health care products: safety, efficacy, interactions with herbs, drugs, and food
3. Latest research in CAM
4. Access to reliable databases, websites, books, journals, continuing education, and other resources on CAM

Knowledge

To be conscious that you are ignorant is a great step to knowledge.

—Benjamin Disraeli (16)

Education serves as the building blocks of knowledge in any practice. Without a standardized system of training, CAM practitioners can have a wide range of variability in their knowledge base, depending on their training. Because CAM providers are often not medically trained, communication barriers naturally exist between conventional and CAM providers *(45)*. Additional challenges include the diversity of concepts of healing, training, and practice within the CAM community; differences in perspective on philosophy, scientific validity, and safety; unavailability of credentialed providers; and ambivalence concerning the value of collaboration with conventional medicine *(46,47)*. Continuing medical education courses that are offered by major medical institutions typically have a tuition that is prohibitive for the CAM practitioners. With such marked differences and limitations, it is understandable why barriers may exist between conventional and CAM providers. (*See* Table 5 for areas of knowledge limitations.)

Attitudes

Human beings, by changing the inner attitudes of their
minds, can change the outer aspects of their lives.

—*William James (16)*

Openness is a two-way street. If the CAM provider wishes
not to collaborate despite all the favorable steps taken by the conventional physician, a fully integrated model cannot be realized.
In our interactions with many CAM practitioners, we have come
across several who may have a personal bias against conventional
medicine. There is neither a will nor a desire to learn about it or
integrate. In contrast, integrative practitioners may not only appreciate the differences, but also the commonality of achieving optimum health in both models. This is in contrast to some CAM
practitioners who may not fathom the importance of integration
because of the fundamental differences between the diagnostics,
therapeutics, and in the way disease and health is perceived in the
two systems.

A similar bias can also be observed in scholarly writings.
Increasingly more articles on the integration of conventional
medicine and CAM are being written in the mainstream medical
literature, but the authors have yet to see the presence of such
concept in the traditional CAM literature.

A good starting place would be to reflect on the existing beliefs that enable and disable such integration. Examples of enabling
elements would be an attitude of openness, willingness to learn,
and the desire and commitment toward open patient communication. Barriers would include lack of knowledge, exclusive attitudes of CAM superiority, and the unwillingness for collaboration.
Once these discoveries are made, then the appropriate resources
would need to be tapped into in order to take realistic steps toward
integration.

Research Skills

Ability is what you're capable of doing. Motivation determines what you do. Attitude determines how well you do it.

—Lou Holtz (1)

It is unfortunate that some clinically astute CAM practitioners do not have a research background. And, of course, excellent researchers do not always have a CAM background. We feel that educational development is needed for both parties to cultivate relationships between them, as the grounds are fertile for research. Through research collaboration, clinical integration may occur. There has to be a systematic way of educating CAM practitioners on basic scientific research that can be achieved through affordable continuing education courses.

Fear of Rejection

It is not rejection itself that people fear; it is the possible consequences of rejection. Preparing to accept those consequences and viewing rejection as a learning experience that will bring you closer to success, will not only help you to conquer the fear of rejection, but help you to appreciate rejection itself.

—Bo Bennett (1)

CAM practitioners too, like patients, are in a vulnerable position when it comes to communication and integration. They, too, perceive the dominance of conventional medicine as one of the major barriers. Our current medical culture and major medical organizations have played a significant role in widening the chasm between CAM and conventional medicine. This fear of rejection is further fueled by CAM practitioners' interaction with patients who either have a personal bias against conventional medicine or have a personal physician who is disapproving of CAM. There may also be a sense of "loss of control" on the part of the CAM practitioner if they were to integrate with modern medicine. There are limited venues, such as the National Education Dialogue (NED), that exist at this point where CAM practitioners and conventional physicians can discuss common educational and communication challenges.

Lack of Infrastructure

The traditional setting of CAM offices is very different from traditional medical practices. Physician practices are usually group or multispecialty with a significant overhead. In the electronic age of e-mails, electronic medical records, and infrastructure support, physicians are well equipped to communicate across disciplines. On the other hand, CAM practitioners generally have a solo practice and a small overhead and not much in the way of infrastructure support to meet the priority of communicating with physicians. Telecommunication is possible but hard to coordinate in busy schedules.

Language Barriers

Man invented language to satisfy his deep need to complain.

—*Lily Tomlin (16)*

In an ideal world, the language of both allopathic medicine and CAM would be the same, however, the real world does not have that provision. It is confusing for physicians to read and understand the language of CAM. We very well recognize the completely different diagnosis and treatment methodologies of the two worlds that we are trying to unite. This language barrier represents the true "culture shock" to the physicians. The marriage of both parties is only possible if and when CAM practitioners learn the language of allopathic medicine and vice versa.

RESPONSIBILITIES OF CAM PRACTITIONERS

If a cooperative, working relationship is developed between conventional and CAM providers, there is an increased possibility of melding conventional medicine and CAM so that the patient and physician can have the best of both worlds in the coming age of global medicine *(25)*.

There has been a call "to create the common ground in health care education which will advance integrated health care." To meet this goal of full integration, national efforts are being made by NED, headed by John Weeks to promote dialogue between CAM and conventional medicine. NED brings together different silos of education and collaborates with other health care disciplines, such as nursing, naturopathic, massage, and chiropractic training. The goals of NED are to discuss shared competencies, shared common values and attitudes, and improve communication and collaboration across disciplines.

NED clearly defines its purpose:

In 2002, the White House Commission on Complementary and Alternative Medicine Policy called for gatherings of leading educators to advance integration of health care education so that, ultimately, the delivery of care can change. The same year, the National Policy Dialogue to Advance Integrated Care independently called for such a dialogue. And, very recently, the Institute of Medicine's report on CAM issued a clarion call for CAM and conventional medicine to work together to change the delivery of health care. The bottom line is this: to integrate care, we must integrate education. *(48)*

Be Enthusiastic About Learning
and Sharing

Just as the call is being made for physicians in conventional medicine to adopt an attitude of enthusiasm about learning and sharing when it comes to CAM, the same necessity holds true for CAM practitioners. There is a plethora of resources available to CAM practitioners, as well as continuing education opportunities to engage in active learning about similarities and differences between CAM and conventional medicine.

Be Open to Integration

In the honor of patient-centered care, more studies are exploring and supporting the need for integrating CAM and conventional medicine. Patients are making choices to use CAM therapies without the involvement of their physicians. Regardless of the professionals' opinions about the other practice, we believe there would be fewer risks and more benefits when working together, with open disclosure about both modalities.

Discuss the Safety and Efficacy
of a Therapy

Patients are entitled to consistency of care, regardless of where they receive it. With this in mind, it is important that CAM practitioners respect patient autonomy in making informed decisions about the use of CAM therapy. Patients need to be made aware of the possible side effects, effectiveness of the therapy to be expected, and any interactions that may occur. This principle reinforces the need for a willingness to nurture an open dialogue about the use of CAM and how it can relate or co-exist simultaneously with conventional medicine.

Set Realistic Goals

It is not realistic to expect a high level of competency in the knowledge and training of conventional medicine, but if CAM practitioners were to adopt the same sense of humility and will-ingness as is expected from conventional physicians and learn about the integration of conventional medicine, CAM, and patient-centered care, then the interconnectivity would benefit patients.

Like physicians, CAM practitioners must also set realistic goals about a particular modality or treatment. Patients' expecta-tions and their prior experiences should be explored. Discussion of a "cure" should occur only if backed by sound scientific data. CAM practitioners should clearly communicate with patients and their physicians about what is possible and what is not possible. If patients bring an unrealistic expectation, the CAM practitioner may wish to defer treatment and refer them back to the patient's physician.

Open Communication With Conventional Physicians

The final key element in the triad of interconnectivity is the connection between CAM practitioners and conventional physi-cians. The challenges involved in this connection have already been discussed, but once identified, efforts can be focused on rec-tifying and overcoming those challenges in the best interests of the patient. Communication is the major gap that needs to be bridged. Although there may be differences in language and philosophical approaches, a synergistic approach supported by communication would be ideal.

CONCLUSION

Patients have demonstrated their desire for resources beyond conventional medicine for prevention, health maintenance, and disease management in their use of CAM. What is the role of the physician in advising patients? With the principle of beneficence in mind, physicians are faced with the challenge of how to deliver quality health care with the patient's best interest at heart. When communicating about CAM, there are multiple barriers that challenge physicians to bridge gaps in the realms of knowledge, cultural, and personal values. Without the successful identification and mending of these barriers, difficulties will ensue when advising—or not advising—patients about the use of CAM.

Physicians need to bear in mind that users of CAM are not necessarily dissatisfied with conventional treatments, but are seeking an orientation toward health and illness that is mindful of the importance of body, mind, and spirit; values the emphasis on treating the whole person; and allows for a more active role in maintaining health *(49)*. Many patients who use CAM therapies do so in conjunction with conventional therapies. Physicians need to be "open-minded skeptics" in advising patients about CAM. They should not be concerned with practicing what is perceived to be conventional vs CAM, or biomedicine vs naturalistic medicine, but with what is truly "good" medicine *(18)*.

There are clear similarities between the challenges facing the three entities in the CAM triad. As previously discussed, there exists a common need for the process of continued learning, application of common standards, attitude of receptivity, and open communication between physicians, patients, and CAM practitioners. There is a need for each to play an active role in the shared process, which requires the acknowledgment, acceptance, and implementation of the responsibilities that we have outlined within this chapter. With a collaborative effort between physicians, patients, and CAM practitioners, an integrative approach toward healing and health promotion can be realized.

Education serves as the foundation for building a concrete relationship between CAM practitioner, patient, and physician. The "triad of interconnectivity" must have open communication channels, carrying knowledge and wisdom from different traditions and cultures. As perfect harmony of mind, body, and spirit is desired for good health, an integrated voice must be orchestrated among physicians, patients, and CAM practitioners to better the quality and delivery of health care.

> A world community can exist only with world communication, which means something more than extensive short-wave facilities scattered about the globe. It means common understanding, a common tradition, common ideas, and common ideals.
>
> —*Robert M. Hutchins*

ACKNOWLEDGMENTS

The authors would like to acknowledge Sudhakar Prasad, PhD and Brian Shelley, MD for their thorough review of the manuscript and helpful comments prior to submission.

REFERENCES

1. Brainy Quote. Available at: http://www.brainyquote.com/quotes/quotes/j/jameshumes154730.html. Accessed June 9, 2006.
2. IOM. Complementary and Alternative Medicine in the United States. Available at: http://www.nap.edu/openbook/0309092701/html/1.html#pagetop. Accessed April 15, 2005.
3. Anonymous. New alternative medicine guide launched amidst increasing reports of adverse reactions. Bulletin of the World Health Organization 2004;82(8):635–636.
4. Kessler RC, Davis RB, Foster DF, et al. Long-term trends in the use of complementary and alternative medical therapies in the United States. Ann Intern Med 2001;135(4):262–268.
5. Eisenberg DM, Kessler RC, Foster C, Norlock FE, Calkins DR, Delbanco TL. Unconventional medicine in the United States. Prevalence, costs, and patterns of use. N Engl J Med 1993;328(4):246–252.

6. Barnes PM, Powell-Griner E, McFann K, Nahin RL. Complementary and alternative medicine use among adults: United States, 2002. Adv Data May 27 2004(343):1–19.

7. Herman CJ, Allen P, Hunt WC, Prasad A, Brady TJ. Use of complementary therapies among primary care clinic patients with arthritis. Prev Chronic Dis [serial online]. Available at: http://www.cdc.gov/pcd/issues/2004/oct/03_0036.htm. Accessed October 2004.

8. Ernst E. Complementary Medicine: An Objective Appraisal. Oxford, UK: Butterworth-Heinemann; 1996.

9. Astin JA. Why patients use alternative medicine: results of a national study. JAMA 1998;279(19):1548–1553.

10. Miller LG. Herbal medicinals: selected clinical considerations focusing on known or potential drug–herb interactions. Arch Intern Med 1998;158(20):2200–2211.

11. Eisenberg DM, Davis RB, Ettner SL, et al. Trends in alternative medicine use in the United States, 1990–1997: results of a follow-up national survey. JAMA 1998;280(18):1569–1575.

12. Eisenberg DM. Advising patients who seek alternative medical therapies. Ann Intern Med 1997;127(1):61–69.

13. Borkan J, Neher JO, Anson O, Smoker B. Referrals for alternative therapies. J Fam Pract 1994;39(6):545–550.

14. NCCAM. Expanding Horizons of Health Care. Available at: http://nccam.nih.gov/about/plans/2005/strategicplan.pdf. Accessed April 15, 2005.

15. Miller FG, Emanuel EJea. Ethical issues concerning research in complementary and alternative medicine. JAMA 2004;291(5):599–604.

16. The Quotations Page. Available at http://www.quotationspage.com/. Accessed June 9, 2006.

17. Wetzel MS, Eisenberg DM, Kaptchuk TJ. Courses involving complementary and alternative medicine at US medical schools. JAMA 1998;280(9):784–787.

18. Perlman AI, Eisenberg DM, Panush RS. Talking with patients about alternative and complementary medicine. Rheum Dis Clin North Am 1999;25(4):815–822.

19. Leading Thoughts. Available at http://www.leadershipnow.com/listeningquotes.html. Access June 9, 2006.

20. Maynard DW, Heritage J. Conversation analysis, doctor–patient interaction and medical communication. Med Educ 2005;39(4):428–435.
21. Sierpina V. Intergrative Health Care: Complementary and Alternative Therapies for the Whole Person. Philadelphia, PA: FA Davis Co., 2001.
22. Stone J, Matthews J. Complementary Medicine and the Law. Oxford: Oxford University Press, 1996.
23. Chan PS, Wong MM. Physicians and complementary-alternative medicine: training, attitudes, and practices in Hawaii. Hawaii Med J 2004;63(6):176–181.
24. Ziment I, Tashkin DP. Alternative medicine for allergy and asthma. J Allergy Clin Immunol 2000;106(4):603–614.
25. Jonas W. Evaluating integrative medicine (a physician's guide to advising patients). Hippocrates. November 2000:19–21.
26. Burstein HJ. Discussing complementary therapies with cancer patients: what should we be talking about? J Clin Oncol 2000; 18(13):2501–2504.
27. Frenkel M, Arye EB. The growing need to teach about complementary and alternative medicine: questions and challenges. Acad Med 2001;76(3):251–254.
28. Adler SR. Disclosing complementary and alternative medicine use in the medical encounter: a qualitive study in women with breast cancer. J Fam Pract 1999;13(2):214–222.
29. Mackenzie G, Parkinson M, Lakhani A, Pannekoek H. Issues that influence patient/physician discussion of complementary therapies. Patient Educ Couns 1999;38(2):155–159.
30. Crellin J, Fernando A. Professionalism and Ethics in Complementary and Alternative Medicine. Binghamton, NY: The Haworth Integrative Healing Press; 2002.
31. Corbin Winslow L, Shapiro H. Physicians want education about complementary and alternative medicine to enhance communication with their patients. Arch Intern Med 2002;162(10):1176–1181.
32. Weiger WA, Smith M, Boon H, Richardson MA, Kaptchuk TJ, Eisenberg DM. Advising patients who seek complementary and alternative medical therapies for cancer. Ann Intern Med Online 2002;137(11):889–903.

33. Kaegi E. A patient's guide to choosing unconventional therapies. CMAJ 1998;158(9):1161–1165.
34. Bennett J, Brown CM. Use of herbal remedies by patients in a health maintenance organization. J Am Pharm Assoc 2000; 40(3):353–358.
35. Fearon J. Complementary therapies: knowledge and attitudes of health professionals. Paediatr Nurs 2003;15(6):31–35.
36. Giordano J, Boatwright D, Stapleton S, Huff L. Blending the boundaries: steps toward an integration of complementary and alternative medicine into mainstream practice. J Altern Complement Med 2002;8(6):897–906.
37. Brooks PM. Undergraduate teaching of complementary medicine. Med J Aust 2004;181(5):275.
38. Barker S. "I wished I was the patient." An evaluation of a complementary medicine module for third year medical students. Med Educ 2000;34:159.
39. Sikand A, Laken M. Pediatricians' experience with and attitudes toward complementary/alternative medicine. Arch Pediatr Adolesc Med 1998;152(11):1059–1064.
40. Hall J, Bulik R, Sierpina V. Community preceptors' attitudes toward and practices of complementary and alternative medicine: a Texas survey. Tex Med 2003;99(5):50–53.
41. Hadley SK, Petry JJ. Medicinal herbs: a primer for primary care. Hosp Pract (Off Ed). 1999;34(6):105–106, 109–112, 115–106 passim.
42. Davis RH, Jr., Donnelly RE, Girard SS, Muma RD, Taft JM, Toth SA. The growing presence of complementary and alternative medicine. JAAPA 2000;13(5):89–90, 93–86, 101 passim.
43. AllRefer.com. Alternative Medicine. Available at: http://health.allrefer.com/alternative-medicine/. Accessed April 29, 2005.
44. Alliance IM. Deepening the Quality of the Human Experience in Healthcare. Available at: http://www.integrativemedalliance.org. Accessed April 29, 2005.
45. Ernst E, Cohen MH, Stone J. Ethical problems arising in evidence based complementary and alternative medicine. J Med Ethics 2004;30(2):156–159.

46. Kreitzer MJ, Mitten D, Harris I, Shandeling J. Attitudes toward CAM among medical, nursing, and pharmacy faculty and students: a comparative analysis.[comment]. Altern Ther Health Med 2002;8(6):44–47, 50–43.

47. Curtis P, McDermott J, Gaylord S, et al. Preparing complementary and alternative practitioners to teach learners in conventional health professions.[comment]. Altern Ther Health Med 2002;8(6):54–59.

48. Ostendorf C. Ostendorf to Participate in Integration of Education for Complementary Alternative Medicine and Conventional Medicine. Available at: http://www.lakeside.edu/ostendorf.php.

49. Berman B. Complementary and alternative medicine: is it just a case of more tools for the medical bag? Clin J Pain 2004;20(1):1–2.

5

Patient and Medical Education on Complementary and Alternative Medicine

Sorting It Out

Catherine Leffler, JD

INTRODUCTION

Millions of Americans use complementary and alternative medicine (CAM) therapies, often in the absence of scientific evidence of their safety and effectiveness and, in many cases, without including a medical professional in the decision-making process *(1)*. Depending on how broadly one defines it, between 36 and 62% of the US population now relies on some form of CAM *(2)*. Although annual visits to CAM practitioners now outnumber visits to primary care physicians *(3)*, only 12% of those using CAM therapies seek them through certified or licensed CAM practitioners *(4)*. CAM users are usually paying out of pocket, using one or more alternative therapies on a regular basis in combination with prescription medications, and generally not discussing their CAM use with their physicians *(5)*.

From: *Biomedical Ethics Reviews: Complementary and Alternative Medicine: Ethics, the Patient, and the Physician*
Edited by: L. Snyder © Humana Press Inc., Totowa, NJ

Although the ethical obligation to assist patients in achieving their goals for health and wellness supports providing evidence-based advice when they ask about CAM therapies, the unique way in which the use of alternative therapies has evolved highlights the importance of roles of physicians as health educators and advocates. Widespread self-medication and self-treatment with what are frequently unproven, untested, and unregulated therapies, in combination with potentially incompatible conventional therapies, raise important questions for physicians. How are patients learning about these therapies and are their information sources trustworthy, unbiased, and valid? What are the perceptions or misperceptions they bring to the decision-making process? Are patients aware of the potential adverse health consequences of these self-treatment decisions? Does the physician have an ethical obligation to proactively intervene in this process? If so, what changes are required in medical education to adequately prepare physicians for that role? This chapter examines these questions.

The first part of this chapter looks at the ways in which consumers are drawn to and learn about CAM therapies, the common misconceptions they have about the safety and regulation of CAM products, and the significant risks involved with the prevailing pattern of CAM self-treatment. The second part argues that if physicians have an ethical duty to become proactive guides for patients as they navigate the seas of CAM information, the profession has a corresponding duty to provide a core of CAM training within professional medical education. The next section explores recent developments in CAM instruction within the medical school curricula and suggests a set of core competencies that physicians need to fulfill in order to provide effective, patient-centered care with regard CAM. The fourth section is designed as a resource for health care professionals and their patients, providing a directory of authoritative CAM sources and discussing strategies for critically evaluating CAM information.

PATIENT EDUCATION: OVERWHELMING INFORMATION, MISINFORMATION, AND MISCONCEPTIONS

Evaluating whether, and what type of CAM education physicians need to best serve patients requires examining how patients currently get their CAM information, how the quality of that information varies depending on the source, and the potential for harm when patients make CAM decisions based on poor-quality information. This section examines CAM from the perspective of patient education by exploring the nature, widely disparate quality and impact of the seemingly unlimited CAM information sources available to patients; and by discussing consumer misconceptions about the current safety and regulatory protections in place with regard to CAM.

The hallmark of CAM is heterogeneity, as it encompasses a wide range of systems (e.g., chiropractic, Traditional Chinese Medicine, homeopathy, naturopathy), mind–body interventions (e.g., deep breathing, meditation, massage, relaxation therapy, prayer, and mental healing, etc.), biologically based therapies (e.g., special diets and dietary supplements), and other therapies *(6)*. Patient goals in turning to CAM are varied as well, including improving well-being, promoting health, enhancing performance, preventing disease, relieving symptoms, or curing disease *(7,8)*. The reasons for the dramatic increase in CAM use since the early 1990s are as diverse as the therapies themselves and include a general societal interest in asserting more personal control over health; preferences for a more natural or holistic approach to health and wellness; compatibility with personal beliefs, values and spirituality; belief that CAM therapies in combination with conventional care yield better outcomes; belief that CAM options are more effective in addressing many symptoms of chronic conditions and disabilities; increasing relative costs and lack of coverage for conventional care, and so on *(9–11)*.

The well over 100 million patients* *(12)*, highly motivated by multiple factors to address diverse personal health issues through a wide spectrum of CAM solutions, are at once a population at risk—in need of reliable health information—and a target market for entrepreneurial vendors of alternative therapies. As a result, they must navigate through a sea of information, from thousands of sources, both familiar and unfamiliar, of frequently indiscernible quality and with varied, sometimes hidden agendas.

Overwhelming Information and Misinformation

The informal waves of information are perhaps the most powerful. Consumers say it is family and friends who most frequently prompt them to consider trying CAM and provide information for making decisions about CAM therapies *(10)*. Colleagues, teammates, and classmates engage in casual conversation on a daily basis about the latest product, practice, or regimen for symptom relief, weight loss, performance enhancement, memory improvement, or general well-being. The informal networks that develop among patients and families dealing with complex chronic diseases and disabling conditions share information about alternative therapies *(10)*. Although this information is communicated with the best of intentions, its origin, scientific basis, and veracity are often unknown and impossible to assess. Making treatment decisions based solely on testimonials from family and friends can obviously be risky, as no two individuals have the same physiological or psychological makeup and each person takes a different array of prescription and over-the-counter (OTC) medications. Thus, the health consequences of the same CAM decision by different individuals are unlikely to be equivalent.

---

*Based on 36% of the US population using some form of CAM other than prayer for personal health reasons (*see* ref. *3*) and January 1, 2005 Census bureau US population estimate of 296 million.

Consumers have expressed some preference for purchasing CAM products through pharmacies, particularly if a pharmacist is accessible for consultation *(13)*. Although both the popular media and pharmacists themselves gave the pharmacy profession poor ratings for knowledge about dietary supplements in 1998, the profession subsequently took serious steps to increase its evidence-based knowledge. The curricula at many pharmacy schools have been expanded to cover the topic, relevant continuing pharmacy education is now common, and at least one large pharmacy chain has established an institute that has trained more than 10,000 pharmacists to counsel patients on the safe, effective use of dietary supplements *(14)*. Patients are further protected in dealing directly with a pharmacist in that federal regulation controls the type of printed materials about dietary supplements that pharmacists may provide, prohibiting direct distribution of material that promotes a particular brand or contains false or misleading information *(15)*. The pharmacist's knowledge of a patient's use of prescription drugs and the historic partnership between physician and pharmacist in coordinating patient care are both factors that support relying on a pharmacist as one source of information in making CAM decisions.

Public libraries can be a valuable source of books, journals, and government publications on alternative therapies and on issues such as health care fraud and consumer protection *(10)*. Many libraries can also provide consumers with access to online CAM information sources. The National Library of Medicine at the National Institutes of Health (NIH) in collaboration with its National Network of Libraries of Medicine, makes nationwide training support available to librarians providing health information to the public to help assure consumers access to accurate, trustworthy health information through their public libraries *(16)*.

The popular media provides much of the information on which consumers base their CAM decisions *(17)*, covering CAM from the human interest, consumer health, and consumer protection perspectives. However, the promotion of some CAM products through print advertisements, infomercials, talk shows, and home shopping networks makes it difficult for even sophisticated consumers to differentiate between unbiased, fact-based CAM information and well-disguised marketing presentations. Although some CAM providers subscribe to professional codes of ethics and strive for truth and fairness in promoting their products and services *(18)*, others are more entrepreneurial and the veracity of the promotional information they distribute can often be tainted by profit motive. There is a great deal of money at stake. The dietary supplement industry, for example, grossed almost $18 billion in 2001 *(19)*.

Such economic potential creates intense pressure to reach the largest possible audience with effective, positive product messages. One effective strategy is to place advertising in vehicles that patients trust, cloak it with the legitimacy of science-based consumer health information, play off vulnerable patients' longings for miracle cures and symptom relief, and perpetuate public misconceptions that "natural" means safe *(20)*. For example, one manufacturer promoted its dietary supplement in *Parade*, *Parenting,* and *People* magazines to parents of children with attention deficit hyperactivity disorder as a proven treatment and a natural alternative to Ritalin *(21)*. The manufacturer was eventually cited by the Federal Trade Commission (FTC) for making false claims and the ads were discontinued. Advertising appears in newspapers, magazines, direct mail, pamphlets, and on television and radio *(22)*. Telemarketing and multilevel marketing programs are also key strategies for marketing alternative therapies, especially to vulnerable populations *(20)*.

The internet has become a significant source of health information. More than 44 million households have internet access *(23)*, and more than 73 million US adults use the internet to obtain health-related information *(24)*. A Kaiser Family Foundation national survey of older Americans points to the increasing importance of the internet as a source of health information for this growing segment of the population: 215 of those aged 65 and over and 53% of those aged 50 to 64 search the internet for health information *(25)*. Forty-eight percent of all health information seekers have searched specifically for online information on alternative or experimental treatments or medications *(24)*.

The internet can be a gateway to reliable information, invaluable to patients in making health care decisions. As the final section in this chapter demonstrates, government agencies, academic institutions, professional societies, and other organizations provide a wealth of well-researched, scientifically accurate free online resources on CAM research, providers, services, products and therapies. The nonprofit organizations supporting patients and families confronting specific diseases and conditions can also provide guidance about relevant CAM therapies. The Alzheimer's Association, American Cancer Society, Arthritis Foundation, Asthma and Allergy Foundation of America, Children with Diabetes, and National AIDS Treatment Advocacy Project are just a few of the organizations that provide balanced, unbiased condition-specific information about alternative treatments on their websites. These sites are especially useful in warning patients about popular products that have been proven ineffective or harmful and in providing information about many of the safe, relatively inexpensive self-healing, mind–body CAM interventions that can improve patient quality of life, but that receive little commercial attention.

Unfortunately, the internet is also an easy, cheap, loosely regulated vehicle for the fast, widespread distribution of promotional, potentially biased, misleading, and even fraudulent information. Both legitimate and fraudulent online marketers promote their products through websites, spam, and chatrooms at costs well below those associated with buying ad space or commercial air time in traditional media *(26)*. A 2003 study of internet marketing of herbal supplements illustrates the point. Of the 443 sites examined, 81% made at least one unsubstantiated health claim,

55% claimed to treat, prevent, diagnose, or cure a specific disease, and fewer than half of those making health claims included the required standard Food and Drug Administration (FDA) disclaimer *(19)*. These results are especially disturbing because the study authors used the most common search engines and focused on websites from the first page of search results, paralleling typical consumer research patterns *(24)*.

The prevalence of false and misleading online health information raises particular concerns because of the high degree of trust consumers place in the internet. Seventy-two percent say they believe all or most of the health information they find online; 69% believe they have never found incorrect health information online *(24)*. This discrepancy between overall consumer trust in internet health information and the accuracy and trustworthiness of that information points to the need for physicians to guide and empower patients in making truly informed CAM decisions.

Misconceptions About Inherent Safety and Regulatory Protections

Consumer confidence in making independent decisions to use CAM therapies is no doubt based in part on misconceptions about the degree to which practitioners and manufacturers are regulated. In fact, the licensing of alternative health practitioners is a matter of state law and there is no standardization regarding whether and to what extent a particular CAM practice is regulated. (*See* Chapter 6 on liability and risk management issues and CAM.) Decisions to use dietary supplements (defined in the Dietary Supplement Health and Education Act of 1994 [DSHEA] as "a product, other than tobacco, intended to supplement the diet that bears or contains one or more of the following dietary ingredients: a vitamin; a mineral; an herb or other botanical; an amino acid; a dietary substance for use by man to supplement the diet by increasing total dietary intake; or a concentrate, metabolite, constituent, extract or combination of any ingredient described above

[15]) are based on the prevailing belief that these products are inherently safe. Consumers may equate the label "natural" with safe, and mistakenly believe that if a product is for sale in a grocery, drug or health food store, that there is oversight to ensure that it contains only the ingredient(s) listed on the label in the quantities listed; that the ingredients are pure and effective for the purpose sold; and that the product is safe when used as directed *(27)*.

The DSHEA reflects a compromise between FDA officials looking to protect the public interest by imposing firmer controls, and powerful industry/consumer opposition to those controls *(14)*. Under the DSHEA, the FDA has no jurisdiction to require premarket testing for safety or efficacy and supplement manufacturers are not required to register with the FDA *(28)*. Supplements are not regulated for purity or potency *(15)*. The manufacture of dietary supplements is not strictly regulated. However, mandatory "good manufacturing practices" regarding temperature, sanitation, and equipment maintenance, similar to those in place for OTC drugs, were enacted in 2004 and are expected to be phased in by 2007 *(27)*.

Under the DSHEA, supplements are not considered drugs and are subject only to postmarket safety, efficacy, and labeling oversight. The burden falls on the FDA to prove that a supplement poses a significant health risk before it can take action to interrupt its marketing or restrict its use *(15)*. The postmarket oversight of the safety of dietary supplements depends in large part on the FDA's system for collecting and reviewing adverse event reports *(28)*. Unfortunately, the Office of the Inspector General has determined that the current voluntary adverse event reporting system provides inadequate consumer protection *(29)*. The FDA receives reports of less than 1% of all dietary supplement adverse events and those reports lack adequate medical, product, manufacturer, or consumer information. Consequently, the FDA is rarely equipped to take safety action based on adverse event reports *(28)*.

Misconceptions regarding the safety of alternative treatments and the level of regulatory protections in place combined with the public's growing desire to exercise autonomous control over health care decisions can leave consumers vulnerable to entrepreneurs looking to prey on the most vulnerable among us. Perhaps the most graphic example of this occurred shortly after the events of September 11, 2001, when the FTC uncovered more than 200 sites targeting the public's fears by marketing homeopathic remedies, dietary supplements, and other products as treatments for contamination by biological agents like anthrax or small pox *(30)*. Both the FDA and a broad coalition of trade associations representing the dietary supplement industry confirmed that there was no scientific basis for any of these marketing claims *(30)*.

Especially Vulnerable Populations

Older Americans are drawn to alternative treatments to prevent or treat illness, relieve symptoms of chronic disease, slow aging, improve memory, maintain overall health, and increase energy. Although many alternative treatments may offer symptom relief or improved quality of life for seniors, without appropriate physician guidance this population is especially vulnerable to false claims and the accompanying risk of physical and economic harm. Seniors are more likely to be suffering with multiple chronic conditions requiring several prescription medications. With as many as 40% of seniors taking dietary supplements, there is a substantial ongoing risk of interaction or interference with prescription drugs. Furthermore, some of the most popular supplements may be contraindicated for seniors with some common conditions.

The General Accounting Office reports that senior citizens spend millions of dollars on anti-aging alternative treatments that either make unsubstantiated claims or contain little or none of the active ingredients listed on the label. They frequently use these products instead of OTC or prescription medications and have misconceptions about responsible use, including the belief that following recommended dosage guidelines is unnecessary *(20)*.

At the other end of the spectrum, alternative treatments are becoming an increasingly important issue in pediatrics. Both the American Academy of Pediatrics *(10)* and the National Association of School Nurses *(31)* have issued policy statements. Children and their parents are increasingly being targeted by marketers of alternative treatments, particularly dietary supplements *(31)*. The FTC *(32)* has become particularly concerned about advertisers targeting families coping with attention deficit hyperactivity disorder and obesity and claiming to offer safe, natural alternatives to prescription medications. Pediatricians estimate that as many as 50% of children with autism are using some form of alternative treatment *(10)*.

Both physicians and parents need to be aware of the increasing popularity of dietary supplements for performance enhancement among student athletes. In a 2000 survey of more than 21,000 college athletes acknowledging use of performance enhancing supplements other than multivitamins, 57% stated they began their supplement use in high school and other surveys suggest that steroid-related supplement use is occurring among middle school athletes *(33)*. Internet-savvy students have access to a variety of supplements which marketers claims will enhance athletic performance, some of which pose serious health risks *(34)*.

Perhaps the population most vulnerable to false or misleading promotion of alternative treatments consists of those suffering from serious illnesses such as cancer, AIDs, multiple sclerosis, diabetes, and arthritis and those coping with chronic conditions such as Gulf War syndrome, headache or back pain, for whom conventional therapy has offered only minimal relief. Many of the nonprofit organizations and government health agencies that support patients and physicians dealing with these health problems track relevant alternative treatments, highlighting those that have been proven effective and issuing warnings regarding dangerous or worthless products and services. The last section of this chapter provides resource information for contacting many of these organizations.

THE ETHICAL IMPERITIVE FOR CAM IN MEDICAL EDUCATION

With regard to CAM, physicians should acknowledge that each patient they see is as likely as not to be using one or more CAM therapies, routinely self-medicating or self-treating based on the personal recommendations of friends and family, media reports, advertising or independent research. Unfortunately, the information on which these CAM decisions are based is as likely to be fraudulent as factual, biased as fair, promotional as evidence-based; and few patients have the skills in the scientific method necessary to effectively evaluate conflicting or biased information sources. The CAM treatments they choose may be helpful, neutral, toxic or otherwise harmful, and have the potential to interfere with conventional therapies or to compromise the accuracy of laboratory tests *(35)*. Decisions to pursue alternative therapies are often not fully informed.

These realities create a need for physicians to understand and empower informed patient choices regarding alternative treatments. Physicians must be willing and able to engage patients in routine, open conversation about their use of alternative therapies *(36)*. That will require physicians to become more informed about current CAM therapies and the state of the science of CAM. The ability to steer patients toward reliable sources of unbiased, trustworthy CAM information will require some familiarity with the CAM literature and the internet. Given that patients do not tend to volunteer information about their CAM use, limiting counseling to circumstances when patients raise the issue is not effective.

Implicit in asking patients about their CAM use is the obligation to offer balanced information on the safety, efficacy, risks, and benefits of the therapies they have chosen. Discussions of CAM can reveal patient goals regarding promoting health, prolonging life, alleviating suffering, or re-establishing autonomy, control, or hope. Providing trustworthy referrals or information resources or simply lending an ear can strengthen a therapeutic relationship strained by the limitations of conventional treatments. Training in a patient-centered perspective, strong, clinical communication skills, and a broad overview and knowledge of CAM therapies and reliable CAM information resources will be prerequisites to providing this type of quality care.

CAM in Professional Medical Education

Although there has been substantial movement toward integrating CAM into professional medical education, the extent of that integration varies significantly and the medical profession is far from unanimous in its support. Proponents range from enthusiastic advocates of one, integrative medicine to skeptics favoring only the most rigorous evidence-based reviews of what works and what doesn't *(37)*. The vocal opposition argues that CAM instruction constitutes an inappropriate drain of valuable time and resources from an already overburdened curriculum and that CAM's frequent lack of a scientific evidence base, questionable safety, uneven regulatory and consumer protections, and entrepreneurial foundations makes its integration into medical education a dangerously premature endorsement by the medical profession *(38,39)*. Despite these widely divergent perspectives, medical education must foster the openness and provide the knowledge and skills required for physicians to evaluate CAM therapies and guide patients as appropriate.

The Evolution of CAM in Professional Medical Education

The increase in CAM content within the medical school curricula has paralleled the explosive growth in use of alternative treatments since the mid-1990s. In the 1996–1997 academic year, 46 of 125 US medical schools included CAM topics within required courses *(38).* One year later, 75 schools reported offering CAM-specific electives or covering CAM in required courses. By the 2002–2003 academic year, 98 medical schools reported providing some form of CAM-specific instruction *(18).* There has been a similar rise in the number of US schools offering courses on spirituality in medicine. Seventeen accredited medical schools offered courses on spirituality in 1994. By 1998, that number had increased to 39, and by 2004 courses on spirituality in medicine were available at 84 US medical schools *(40).*

Although these statistics provide some indication of the presence of CAM in the medical curriculum, they provide little insight into course content. Brokaw and colleagues surveyed CAM course directors at US medical schools in 2000–2002 about the details of what was being taught *(41).* Respondents reported on courses taught at 52 US medical schools. The majority of courses were electives, sponsored by clinical departments, and team-taught by CAM practitioners or prescribers to give students a broad CAM overview. This study raised several significant concerns. First, less than 18% of respondents emphasized a critical evaluation of CAM treatments or claims of therapeutic efficacy and only 8.2% mentioned including anything related to evidence-based medicine. More than 78% of the courses were taught by practitioners or prescribers of CAM therapies, suggesting they "may be less inclined to impart a critical perspective based on accepted standards of scientific evidence." Finally, the selection and relative weight of course content seemed more a function of the background and interests of the instructor(s) than of scientific principles *(41).*

One initial area of focus for the National Center for Complementary and Alternative Medicine (NCCAM) was the development of models for incorporating CAM into the curricula of medical, dental, and nursing schools *(42)*. Beginning in 2001, the Center funded 15 five-year projects to encourage new educational approaches to incorporating CAM information into professional school curricula, residency training programs, and continuing medical education. Each of these programs took a different approach to teaching CAM, reflecting the goals and objectives of the particular educational institution and the principal investigators, and the resources available to them. The following are examples of NCCAM funded projects:

- The University of Washington project involves a collaboration with Bastyr University (a school of naturopathic medicine in Seattle) to develop and integrate an interdisciplinary evidence-based CAM curriculum into the existing required courses, create new electives throughout the 4-year program, and foster interdisciplinary student interactions and exploration of similarities and differences between CAM and conventional approaches to healing *(43)*.
- The Tufts University program concentrates on pain, palliative and supportive care, collaborating with the New England School of Acupuncture to focus on East Asian Medicine *(18)*.
- In the Oregon Health and Science University (OHSU) program, a task force of faculty from OHSU, the National College of Naturopathic Medicine, Oregon College of Oriental Medicine and Western States Chiropractic College determined the core objectives for a 4-year curriculum for medical students in CAM, and then embarked on designing, implementing, and evaluating a curriculum to meet those objectives *(44)*.

- The Georgetown University program focuses on aiming the CAM curriculum at all students through required courses and integrating CAM material into basic science courses so that all graduates of the school of medicine will be able to understand CAM advances and advise and communicate with their patients more effectively about CAM *(45)*.
- The American Medical Student Association worked with experts in the field to develop a comprehensive CAM curriculum and then selected six medical schools (University of Connecticut, University of Massachusetts, University of California at Irvine, Kansas City University of Medicine and Biosciences, University of Texas Health Science Center at San Antonio, and Louisiana State University Health Sciences Center) to pilot that curriculum *(46)*.

The University of Arizona has developed a comprehensive Program in Integrative Medicine that encompasses required and elective courses in the College of Medicine, an Integrative Family Medicine Residency, a fellowship program, a research program and a broad catalog of online continuing education courses *(47)*. The Integrative Family Practice Residency program is co-sponsored with the Albert Einstein College of Medicine, the Maine Medical Center, the University of Wisconsin at Madison, the OHSU, and the Middlesex Hospital Family Practice Residency Program, and expands the traditional 3-year family practice residency to 4 years to accommodate training in integrative medicine. Arizona's extensive catalog of online courses in integrative medicine includes a nutrition series (e.g., Nutrition and Cancer, Nutrition and Cardiovascular Health), a comprehensive Clinical Integration series addressing integrating CAM and alternative therapies in the treatment of specific diseases and conditions such as asthma, depression, etc., a Consulting With... series that covers collaborating with CAM professionals for the benefit of patients (e.g., Consulting With Mind–Body Practitioners, Consulting With Homeopaths, Consulting With Energy Medicine Practitioners, etc. *[48]*).

The University of New Mexico (UNM) Health Sciences Center Section of Integrative Medicine provides medical students, residents, faculty and practicing physicians with training in integrative medicine. Medical students have several elective opportunities including "Perspectives in Integrative Medicine" and a 4-week CAM elective as well as exposure to integrative medicine through a selective rotation at the UNM Integrative Medicine Clinic. Resident opportunities for integrative medicine training include grand rounds, an elective integrative medicine rotation and others. The section of Integrative Medicine also sponsors an international biennial continuing medical education conference on integrative medicine *(49)*.

The Department of Family Medicine at the University of Texas Medical Branch at Galveston also has an ambitious program in integrative healthcare. First-year students explore the potential benefits and risks of alternative therapies from a problem-solving perspective in their clinical decision-making course, learning the importance of good medication histories including OTC medications and dietary supplements, and gaining first-hand experience in finding reliable online information sources about CAM therapies. CAM is also integrated into the clinical clerkships and required courses. A fourth-year elective in alternative and integrative medicine combines seminars, a journal club, visits to alternative practitioners, development of a self-care plan, journaling, and participation in reflective and relaxation experiential learning. Selectives enable students to spend time with holistic practitioners, do research projects on basic science in CAM modalities, or explore the legal, ethical, or cultural issues surrounding alternative care. The program also focuses on the importance of ethnic, cultural, and spiritual issues that arise in the clinical setting with regard to CAM. Alternative care is also integrated into residency through presentations during rounds, grand rounds, lectures, ambulatory clinic report, and the like, to introduce tools for practice and resources for patient care *(50)*.

The Harvard Medical School offers an elective in CAM that provides a general introduction to the theory and practice of CAM, requires critical reading of the literature and assessment of the state of CAM science, and involves practice in discussing CAM use with patients. The School of Public Health also offers a course titled Complementary and Alternative Medicine: Health Law and Public Policy. The Harvard Medical School Osher Institute and Division for Research and Education in Complementary and Integrative Medicine, through funding from the NIH, the Medtronic Foundation, and other private sources has developed a model for an integrative care clinical center within a major academic medical center. Although the model center will have multiple goals, the education efforts will be directed toward the interdisciplinary team of conventionally trained physicians, ancillary care providers, and licensed complementary care providers. The first educational program, currently under development, focuses on facilitating the effectiveness of that team and their shared decision making. The center will also serve as a clinical training site for the Osher Institute's NIH-supported fellows in complementary and integrative medicine *(51)*.

Several innovative educational initiatives in integrative pediatrics evolved out of an interdisciplinary collaboration among physicians, pharmacists, dieticians, nurses, medical librarians and web specialists from the Children's Hospital Boston, Harvard Medical School, Boston Medical Center, Massachusetts College of Pharmacy and Health Sciences and the Dana Farber Cancer Institute with funding support from the National Library of Medicine and the NCCAM. One of the group's earliest initiatives was a voluntary e-mail education program on herbs and dietary supplements. On a weekly basis, the more than 500 participating dietitians, pharmacists, physicians and nurses received a series of interactive, case-based learning modules via e-mail, followed by multiple-choice questions with appropriate feedback and e-mail discussion. This program was extremely well received, eliciting more than 300 more participants than expected. Participants completed the program despite the fact that no continuing education or other formal credit was provided. The participants praised the internet as an effective, inexpensive means of delivering case-based CAM instruction *(52)*.

The same group started the Pediatric Integrative Medicine Education (PIME) project through the NCCAM education grant program discussed previously. The project focused on faculty development, a fellows program, and medical student and resident education. The most innovative aspects of the project are the faculty development program and the creation of the HolisticKids.org website to educate residents in integrative pediatric medicine. Kemper and colleagues developed a voluntary six-seminar faculty development program in integrative pediatrics that drew faculty from several pediatric programs in the Boston area including the Harvard Medical School, the Boston Combined Pediatric Residency Program, and the Pediatric Fellowship Program at Boston Children's Hospital *(53)*. Each session involved a pretest of knowledge and confidence on the session topic, background reading, and discussion questions as preparation, a case-based experiential seminar, and a post-session test and questionnaire. The program goal was "to improve key faculty members' knowledge, attitudes and communications skills about 4 [*sic*] types of CAM therapies: herbs and dietary supplements, mind–body therapies, massage, and acupuncture." Although the number of participants in the first series was small, the impact was significant. The pre- and post-session tests demonstrated substantial CAM knowledge gains and increased confidence in discussing the covered CAM therapies with patients, students, trainees, and colleagues. Participants reported changes in clinical and teaching practices as a result of the program, including increasing the frequency of CAM discussions with patients and students, initiating CAM discussions rather than waiting for patients or parents to do so, and taking specific steps to teach and disseminate course materials. Participants demonstrated leadership by incorporating integrative medicine within their own curricula *(52)*.

Recognizing that residents frequently turn to the internet as a key resource for professional development, the PIME team created the HolisticKids.org Website to provide an educational source for quality information on CAM in pediatrics *(54)*. The development team included a pediatrician, a pharmacist, a medical librarian, and a web specialist, among others *(52)*. The site is divided into the following four key areas:

1. The *overview of therapies* area provides a brief description of each CAM modality with links to carefully selected websites for more in depth information.
2. The *teaching toolbox* is built around a list of common pediatric problems, allowing the visitor to select a problem and then download the corresponding chapter from *The Holistic Pediatrician*, or view related articles from PubMed, lists of appropriate OTC and prescription medications, and CAM interventions. For some illnesses, case studies are also provided.
3. The *information and resources* section provides access to a local drug information center that responds to inquiries on CAM therapies, includes a list of local libraries, their access policies and CAM holdings, links to two comprehensive CAM information resources, and provides an up-to-date listing of educational opportunities related to CAM.
4. The *practitioners* area provides several alternative methods of searching for local alternative medicine practitioners. This section has become the most frequently accessed part of the site.

This overview of ongoing efforts to integrate CAM into the medical education curriculum, although not exhaustive, has touched on undergraduate, graduate and continuing medical education at both public and private institutions in all areas of the country. Clearly, there is little consensus on what should be taught, how it should be taught, or when it should be taught. It does appear that in many instances, consistent with the observations of Brokaw and colleagues *(41)*, the subject matter for many courses and programs seems to be driven more by the particular CAM resources available to the institution and/or by the interests of leading faculty members rather than by the academic standards applied to conventional courses. The most innovative and comprehensive programs seem to develop when interdisciplinary collaborative teams of highly motivated individuals evolve through their common interest in integrative medicine.

Recommendations, Guidelines, and Core Competencies

Educating physicians in CAM theory, practice, and patient counseling is still a relatively new and evolving process. One step in that process is the organized effort by leaders in the profession to develop recommendations, guidelines, or core competencies in an effort to standardize this aspect of medical education. Several groups have begun working in this arena.

The Society of Teachers of Family Medicine Group on Alternative Medicine issued *Suggested Curriculum Guidelines on Complementary and Alternative Medicine* in 1999 as recommendations for those wishing to incorporate CAM into residency training *(55)*. The guidelines focus on the attitudes, knowledge, and skills residents must acquire to become "unbiased advocates and advisors to patients about CAM." With regard to attitudes, the guidelines call specifically for educating residents to respect the ethnic and cultural influences that may draw patients to alternative care, to discuss use of CAM as a necessary part of practicing patient-centered medicine, and to develop a willingness to seek out and collaborate with qualified CAM practitioners to ensure patient access to appropriate care. The knowledge requirements include the prevalence and patterns of CAM use; legal issues (licensing, credentialing, referral, collaboration, documentation); reimbursement issues; application of evidence-based medicine principles to the study of CAM; the theory, philosophy, common clinical application, and indication for referral; potential adverse effects; current research evidence for efficacy and cost effectiveness; and one reputable reference source for more information for each major category of CAM. The skills component calls for residents to develop the ability to ask patients about their CAM use in an open, nonthreatening manner, to gather information on safety, efficacy and cost of CAM interventions, and to clearly communicate it to the patient to facilitate informed CAM decisions, and to interact collegially with CAM practitioners to achieve quality patient care.

The White House Commission on Complementary and Alternative Medicine in 2002 reviewed the status of professional medical education regarding CAM at that time and made the following recommendations.

- CAM taught within conventional medical education should be (a) incorporated into required courses, not relegated to electives, (b) evidence-based, (c) include the conceptual basis of CAM practices, (d) provide a critical review of safety and efficacy, and (e) include experiential opportunities in mind–body therapies.
- The education of CAM and conventional practitioners should "ensure public safety, improve health and increase the availability of qualified and knowledgeable CAM and conventional practitioners and enhance the collaboration among them."

- Medical schools, postgraduate training programs, and continuing education programs should develop core CAM curricula to prepare conventional physicians to discuss CAM with patients and support informed choices about CAM.
- CAM and medical education should facilitate communication and foster collaboration between CAM and conventional students, practitioners, researchers, educators, institutions, and organizations *(4)*.

Following their 2002 examination of the content being offered by CAM course directors at US medical schools, Brokaw and his colleagues stated that medical students must be trained to "consider the evidence for or against a given CAM therapy, critically evaluate the source and quality of the supporting data, and appraise the therapy's potential for harm when used alone or in combination with conventional therapies." They offered medical schools three suggestions for achieving those educational goals:

- Emphasize critical evaluation of the scientific literature.
- Enlist faculty from the basic science departments with expertise in experimental design and statistical analysis to help teach critical perspective and foster appreciation for medicine's scientific basis.
- Avoid advocacy of unproven therapies by holding CAM courses to the same academic standards as other courses and requiring curriculum committee approval *(41)*.

In 2003, Wetzel et al. reviewed the current state of CAM education in US medical schools and outlined a 10-step plan for educating physicians who are "knowledgeable and comfortable talking with patients about the entire range of allopathic and complementary therapies, familiar with local CAM practitioners and offerings, dedicated to helping their patients gain and maintain health through one inclusive medicine." The steps include the following:

- Define a core curriculum in CAM, starting with the most heavily used therapies, as revealed by patients in major studies and including dietary supplements and herbal remedies owing to the safety issues.
- Teach one, evidence-based medicine, teach students to be unbiased evaluators of the evidence, to find information about clinical trials, to be discerning, critical readers of all scientific literature, to examine the methods of studies, to understand the possible placebo effect and other influences, and so on.
- Create opportunities for cross-fertilization by incorporating an exchange rotation or externship for medical students with schools of chiropractic, acupuncture, mind–body therapy, therapeutic massage, naturopathy, Traditional Chinese Medicine, and so on.
- Offer a well-designed elective.
- Include an experiential component *(38)*.

Although the core competencies outlined in the Institute of Medicine's (IOM) 2003 report *Health Professions Education: A Bridge to Quality* were originally drafted in relation to conventional medicine, they are especially relevant to the physician's role in advising patients on alternative care. They stress the need to educate physicians to provide patient-centered care, which requires "the ability to communicate with patients in a shared and fully open manner; take into account the patient's individuality, emotional needs, values and life issues; and enhance prevention and health promotion" *(56)*. In its 2005 report, the IOM Committee on the Use of Complementary and Alternative Medicine by the American Public recommended that "health profession schools (e.g., schools of medicine, nursing, pharmacy, and allied health) incorporate sufficient information about CAM into the standard curriculum at the undergraduate, graduate, and post-graduate levels to enable licensed professionals to competently advise their patients about CAM" *(18)*. The committee also stressed the importance of evaluating all CAM educational programs according to the same standards applied to other medical school curricula topics.

The Consortium of Academic Health Centers for Integrative Medicine (CAHCIM) is a collaboration of 23 academic medical centers whose mission is "to help transform health care through rigorous scientific studies, new models of clinical care, and innovative educational programs that integrate biomedicine, the complexity of human beings, the intrinsic nature of healing and the rich diversity of therapeutic systems." During 2002–2003, the CAHCIM Education Working Group defined a set of curriculum guidelines in integrative medicine for medical schools. Endorsed by the CAHCIM Steering Committee in 2003, the guidelines outline core competencies in terms of values, knowledge, attitudes, and skills. The values competencies address issues including (a) the physician's philosophy and perspective on illness, (b) the definition of professionalism as it supports relationships within the health care team and with patients, (c) the importance of recognizing the pursuit of meaning as fundamental to the healing process for both patient and physician, (d) the importance of recognizing the multiple factors that influence health and healing, and so on. The knowledge competencies include the ability to (a) discuss how cultural, ethnic, personal, and spiritual beliefs impact one's experience of disease and treatment; (b) discuss major strengths and weaknesses of conventional medical knowledge in health care; (c) distinguish between curing and healing; (d) describe the prevalence and patterns of CAM use in the patient's community; (e) describe the basic concepts of the most commonly used CAM modalities; identify reputable information resources for CAM and IM; and (f) discuss the current regulatory status of dietary supplements. The attitudes competencies include

(a) the ability to demonstrate respect for the influence a patient's cultural, ethnic, spiritual, and personal beliefs have on clinical decision making and the experience of health and illness; (b) awareness of how one's personal beliefs impact treatment recommendations; (c) respect for the strengths and limitations of applying evidence-based medicine principles to the circumstances of particular patients; (d) respect for the potential of varied healing methods for the treatment of certain conditions; and (e) awareness of the importance of self-care to physician well-being and as an example to promote patient self-care. The skills competencies include a demonstrated ability to (a) assist patients in creating a self-care plan; (b) communicate effectively with patients about all aspects of health and illness, including psychosocial, spiritual, and physical history, and use of CAM; (c) collaborate effectively with all members of the interdisciplinary care team to facilitate quality patient care; and (d) use evidence-based principles to analyze integrative medicine approaches *(55)*.

Concluding Thoughts on CAM in Medical Education

As the overview just presented demonstrates, substantial progress has been made in integrating CAM subject matter into all levels of professional medical education. The extent and character of that integration varies from institution to institution and from department to department within institutions. Although some argue for consistency or standardization in educational approach *(58)*, the diversity in budgetary constraints, available CAM resources, clinical and academic priorities, and faculty strengths and limitations argue strongly for flexibility in how CAM is integrated into the curriculum. The programs discussed range from small-scale and focused, involving the introduction of a single CAM elective to the comprehensive integrative medicine programs in Arizona, Massachusetts, and Texas spanning medical school, residency, continuing medical education, and faculty development. All represent progress toward preparing physicians to provide more patient-centered care.

The crucial question is as follows, "What is the core content medical students, residents, faculty and practicing physicians must master to be prepared to support patients in making fully informed decisions about alternative treatments?" The guidelines, core competencies, and recommendations discussed here address this question in great detail. In a nutshell, it can be summarized as follows:

1. Attitudes and Understanding: Medical students, physicians in training, and practicing physicians must develop an understanding of the spiritual, cultural, ethnic, and personal health values that draw patients to alternative treatments.
2. Knowledge: Physicians should be able to demonstrate knowledge of the most commonly used CAM modalities, their benefits, risks, interactions with conventional treatments, reputable practitioners, and how they are regulated/licensed in the physician's state.
3. Research and Critical Evaluation: Physicians must be skilled at researching current studies and other relevant reliable literature on CAM therapies and critically evaluating the evidence, risks, benefits, interactions with conventional therapies, costs in order to draw their own informed conclusions and to support patients in making fully informed decisions.
4. Communication Skills: Physicians must develop communication skills necessary to proactively raise the question of CAM use or interest in a manner that facilitates open discussion and be able to appropriately discuss the evidence with patients during the decision-making process.

Much has been said about teaching one integrated medicine *(38)*. Given that the Cochrane Collaboration's subscriber-based database maintains information on more than 5000 randomized controlled trials involving CAM and that the number of peer-reviewed studies of alternative therapies is growing monthly, it may be appropriate to incorporate both CAM and allopathic medicine within the same curriculum and to hold them both to the same level of critical evaluation. First-year medical students could be taught, in the same course, to critically evaluate both alternative and allopathic medical literature, to examine study methods, and to consider the placebo effect and other influences. Regardless of how CAM is treated in the rest of the curriculum, introducing it in this way will place it in the appropriate context early in the aspiring physician's academic career.

One subject area that was rarely specifically stressed for inclusion in the curriculum is training in identification and evaluation of online health information resources. As previously discussed, patients obtain much of their information about both CAM and traditional therapies from the internet, and the quality of that information is variable to say the least. Physicians should help them sort through that information and be able to point them toward reliable sources of online information. Furthermore, physicians who require additional information on therapies about which their patients have inquired will often find the internet their most expedient source. Training on efficient use of the internet as a medical research tool can benefit medical students, residents, and practicing physicians alike. Collaboration with a medical librarian and a web specialist might be helpful in designing an educational session to address this topic. The final section in this chapter can also serve as a resource.

Given the level of effort already invested in integrating CAM into medical education, institutions, or departments looking to embark on new or expanded CAM education, initiatives should begin by networking with colleagues who have been most active in the field. The NCCAM website maintains information on the Center's medical education grantees for this purpose. The authors and programs referenced in this section provide another resource. In addition, the University of Texas Medical Branch Complementary and Alternative Medicine Project maintains a CAM Education Series on its website that includes 17 articles on CAM educational initiatives across the country, each providing the names of key faculty members *(59)*. Finally, institutions with limited resources can look to the faculty development program instituted early in the history of Boston's PIME project as a way of leveraging those resources by cultivating CAM-capable faculty throughout the conventional curriculum.

FINDING AND EVALUATING CAM INFORMATION

Physicians and patients frequently have a need for information on alternative therapies. Physicians may be seeking ways to relieve symptoms for which conventional treatments offer little help or cause intolerable side effects. A patient pursuing CAM as part of a strategy for achieving overall health goals might research multiple potential therapies before making a decision. That research should be targeted to unbiased, science-based authorities and should include thoughtful discussion with the patient's primary care physician. As previously discussed, the available CAM information sources are virtually unlimited, and range from helpful to harmful and fact-based to fraudulent. This section is intended to provide patients and health care professionals alike with a brief directory of sources of authoritative information on CAM therapies, disease-specific CAM guidance, research trials and results, and risks and warnings, and to provide a quick guide to evaluating the CAM information they encounter.

CAM Information Resources for Patients and Health Professionals

This section provides a directory of reliable information resources covering CAM from a variety of perspectives. Each source name is followed by the link to the website or CAM-specific web page.

Federal Government Resources

NATIONAL CENTER FOR COMPLEMENTARY AND ALTERNATIVE MEDICINE (http://nccam.nih.gov/)

Congress established NCCAM within the NIH in 1998 and charged it with exploring CAM in the context of rigorous science; focusing on basic scientific and clinical research in CAM, training and career development for CAM researchers; and public and professional outreach and education regarding scientifically proven, evidence-based CAM practices.

The NCCAM website provides a wealth of information for consumers, health care professionals, and researchers, including the following: fact sheets on specific CAM therapies; fact sheets on CAM for specific diseases or conditions; pamphlets titled "Considering CAM Therapies?"; "Choosing A CAM Service Provider"; "Financial Issues in CAM"; alerts and advisories; and grant information for researchers.

The website also provides direct search access to CAM on PubMed, a collection of more than 220,000 citations accessed through the PubMed database and to the Combined Health Information Database (CHID), which includes health-related materials not available in other government databases.

The NCCAM Public Information Clearinghouse is the public's point of contact for scientifically based information on CAM. The Clearinghouse can be accessed online at http://nccam.nih.gov/nccam/fcp/clearinghouse/. Inquiries are also accepted by phone, fax, or e-mail.

Tel: 1-888-644-6226; outside United States: (301) 519-3153
Fax: 1-866-464-3616 (toll free)
TTY: 1-866-464-3615 for the hearing impaired (toll free)
E-mail: info@nccam.nih.gov.

OFFICE OF CANCER COMPLEMENTARY AND ALTERNATIVE MEDICINE (OCCAM; http://www.cancer.gov/cam/)

The OCCAM was established in 1998 within the National Cancer Institute (NCI) to coordinate and enhance the activities of the institute with regard to CAM. The OCCAM Research Development and Support Program stimulates research in cancer CAM. The Practice Assessment Program reviews data on cancer patients treated with unconventional and CAM therapies and allows practitioners to share their successes and have them evaluated by experts in both conventional and alternative medicine. The Communications Program disseminates information about NCI CAM initiatives, funding opportunities, clinical trials, and educational materials via the OCCAM website.

NATIONAL INSTITUTE OF DIABETES AND DIGESTIVE AND KIDNEY DISEASES (NIDDK)

NATIONAL DIABETES INFORMATION CLEARINGHOUSE, CAM THERAPIES FOR DIABETES (http://diabetes.niddk.nih.gov/dm/pubs/alternativetherapies/)

This web page provides a brief discussion about the current state of the science on some of the CAM therapies most frequently used by diabetes patients. It also provides direct links to the NCCAM and to an automatic search on "Complimentary and Alternative Medical Therapies for Diabetes" on the CHID, which is produced by the health-related agencies of the US government.

NIH OFFICE OF DIETARY SUPPLEMENTS (ODS; http://dietary-supplements.info.nih.gov/)

The Office of Dietary Supplements is charged with conducting and coordinating research within NIH relating to dietary supplements, collecting and compiling results of research on dietary supplements, and advising the secretary and assistant secretary of health, the directors of the CDC and the NIH and the commissioner of the FDA on issues relating to dietary supplements. The ODS website provides access to a variety of information on dietary supplement use and safety; reports on research and recommendations; FDA warnings; FTC false advertising claims; and NIH and

Department of Agriculture databases. The ODS also makes the following publications available on its website to assist consumers in making informed decisions regarding dietary supplements:

- The Savvy Supplement User (FDA)
- Tips for Older Supplement Users (FDA)
- How to Spot Health Care Fraud (FDA)
- How to Evaluate Health Information on the Internet: Questions and Answers (ODS).

NATIONAL INSTITUTE ON AGING: AGEPAGE
(http://www.niapublications.org/engagepages/healthqy.asp)

This site warns seniors about the common problem of false health claims in advertising or marketing schemes. Identifies red flags to watch for, provides tips for protecting against health scams, and identifies resources to for additional information or obtain assistance with being victimized by a health scam.

CLINICALTRIALS.GOV (http://www.clinicaltrials.gov/)

This site provides a complete listing of all clinical trials sponsored by the NIH. To find a complete listing of clinical trials in CAM, search under the term "alternative medicine."

FOOD AND DRUG ADMINISTRATION CENTER FOR FOOD SAFETY AND APPLIED NUTRITION; OFFICE OF NUTRITIONAL PRODUCTS LABELING AND DIETARY SUPPLEMENTS (ONPLDS; www.cfsan.fda.gov/~dms/supplmnt.html)

The ONPLDS within the FDA is responsible for regulation, education, and outreach regarding dietary supplements. The website provides access to up-to-date warnings and safety information, adverse event reporting information, an electronic newsletter, frequently requested information, and a variety of consumer education publications.

THE FTC BUREAU OF CONSUMER PROTECTION
(http://www.ftc.gov/bcp/menu-health.htm)

The FTC Bureau of Consumer Protection is charged with protecting the public against false advertising and publishes consumer education materials on a variety of health care fraud issues through its website. Those publications include *"Miracle" Health Claims: Add a Dose of Skepticism*; *Offers to Treat Biological Threats: What You Need to Know*; *Promotions for Kids' Dietary Supplements Leave a Sour Taste*; *The Truth About Impotence Treatment Claims;* and *Tipping the Scales? Weight Loss Ads Found Heavy on Deception.*

FIRSTGOV FOR CONSUMERS — HEALTH
(http://www.consumer.gov/health.htm)

This comprehensive site provides links, by topic, to health-related US government resources on the internet.

Academic Medical Centers

COLUMBIA UNIVERSITY, RICHARD & HINDA ROSENTHAL CENTER FOR CAM)
http://www.rosenthal.hs.columbia.edu)

This center is dedicated to contributing to the informed research and practice of CAM and to fostering a more comprehensive and inclusive medical system. It focuses on problems in women's health and aging. The center also includes the Carol Ann Schwartz Initiative CAM Cancer Information Center to serve as an information source on CAM in cancer treatment for professionals and patients.

DUKE COMPREHENSIVE CANCER CENTER
(http://cancer.duke.edu/pated/cam.asp)

The Duke Comprehensive Cancer Center makes *A Cancer Patient's Guide to Complementary and Alternative Medicine* available for printing. It provides an overview of CAM, includes a section on organizational, internet, and other CAM information sources, explores the integration of CAM and conventional approaches to health care for cancer patients, and provides a series of CAM information sheets covering topics such as professional degrees and titles of alternative practitioners; education, training, licensing, and accreditation of health care practitioners; how to be prepared before, during, and after appointments with a health care provider; and so on

MAYO CLINIC
(http://www.mayoclinic.com)

By choosing the Complementary and Alternative Medicine Center from the Mayo Clinic home page, patients and physicians move to the Mayo CAM page where they can choose to learn about CAM in general, explore specific CAM modalities, research alternative treatment options for specific health problems, and more.

OREGON HEALTH AND SCIENCE UNIVERSITY
(http://www.ohsuhealth.com/htaz/cam)

This site provides general CAM information, a CAM glossary, a section on safety and risks, online resources, and a link to alternative therapies for pediatric cancer.

PIME PROJECT (http://www.holistickids.org/index.html)

The PIME project is a center of excellence project of education and research in the provision of integrative health care to children. Based at Children's Hospital, Boston, PIME is sponsored by a grant from the NCCAM and involves a collaborative effort with Harvard Medical School, the Massachusetts College of Pharmacy, and Boston Medical Center.

UNIVERSITY OF MARYLAND SCHOOL OF MEDICINE CENTER FOR INTEGRATIVE MEDICINE
(http://www.compmed.umm.edu/index.html)

This is the website for the University of Maryland School of Medicine's interdepartmental center for research, patient care, education, and training regarding CAM. The website provides two comprehensive guides available online:*Complementary Medicine Resources for Health Professionals and Researchers* and *Consumer Guide to Internet Resources in CAM*.

The center is also the coordinator of the Complementary Medicine Field of the Cochrane Collaboration, which is dedicated to promoting and facilitating the production of high-quality systematic reviews of the scientific evidence in CAM topics. Although the Cochrane Library is a subscription service available on CD-Rom and on the internet, the Cochrane Complementary Medicine Controlled Clinical Trials Registry is accessible for searching through this site at http://wwwcompmed.umm.edu/cochrane/field.html.

UNIVERSITY OF TEXAS MD ANDERSON CANCER CENTER COMPLEMENTARY/ INTEGRATIVE MEDICINE EDUCATION RESOURCES
(http://www.mdanderson.org/departments/cimer)

This website is designed to help cancer patients and physicians responsibly integrate CAM into cancer care. It provides evidenced-based reviews of CAM therapies, alerts from the FDA on herb and dietary supplement interactions with drugs, and other advisories, other relevant resources and links, and so on.

UNIVERSITY OF TEXAS MEDICAL BRANCH INTEGRATIVE HEALTH CARE WEBSITE
(http://cam.utmb.edu/default.asp)

This site is dedicated to providing health care professionals, students, and the public with reliable, evidence-based, authoritative information on alternative therapy topics for educational purposes. In addition to providing extensive information on CAM, the site is an outstanding resource for medical educators, providing detailed curricula, syllabi, lectures, web-based cases, and progress notes on CAM programs at other medical schools.

Nonprofit Organizations Providing CAM Guidance to Patients and Health Professionals

The following is a list of nonprofit organizations and their websites.

- The Alzheimer's Association (http://www.alz.org/Health/Treating/treatments.asp)
- The American Cancer Society (http://www.cancer.org/docroot/ETO/ETO_5.asp)
- The Arthritis Foundation (http://www.arthritis.org/conditions/alttherapies/nature.asp)
- Asthma and Allergy Foundation of America (http://aafa.org/display.cfm?id=9&sub=21&cont=293)

- Autism Society of America (http://www.autism-society.org/ site/PageServer?pagename=Com-plementaryApproaches)
- Diabetes123 and Children with Diabetes (http://www. diabetes123.com/clinic/alternative_concerns.htm)
- National Multiple Sclerosis Society (http://www.national mssociety.org/spotlight-cam.asp)
- The National Aids Treatment Advocacy Project (http:// www.natap.org/)

Evaluating CAM Information

This section outlines a process for evaluating online CAM resources and identifies terms, phrases, and communication strategies that are often warning signs of potentially fraudulent information. It also introduces the Health on the Net Foundation (HON), an international nonprofit initiative that has developed a code of conduct for providing health information on the internet. Although the guidance provided focuses specifically on evaluating online CAM information, many of the underlying principles can be applied to assess the credibility of CAM information found in television, radio, and print media.

Evaluating Health Resources on the Web

As previously discussed, there is a vast amount of health-related information available on the internet. Several credible initiatives have been undertaken to establish criteria for evaluating the quality of that information *(60)*. The 10-question evaluation process outlined below is adapted from the NCCAM Fact Sheet *10 Things to Know About Evaluating Medical Resources on the Web (61)*.

1. Who runs the site? Any good health-related website should make it easy to learn who is responsible for the site and its information. The name of the sponsoring organization should be clearly marked on every major page of the site, along with a link to the organization's home page.

2. Who pays for the site? The source of a website's funding should be clearly stated or readily apparent. For example, web addresses ending in ".gov" denote a federal government-sponsored site; ".edu" indicates an educational institution; ".org" is often used by noncommercial or nonprofit entities, and ".com" usually denotes a commercial organization. How does the site cover its costs? Does it sell advertising? Is it sponsored by a drug company? The source of funding can affect what and how the content is presented.

3. What is the purpose of the site? This question is related to who runs and pays for the site. Many sites have an "About This Site" or "About Us" link. If it is there, use it. The purpose of the site should be clearly stated to assist in the evaluation of the trustworthiness of the information provided on it.

4. Where does the information come from? Many health/medical sites post information collected from other websites or sources. If the person or organization in charge of the site did not create the information, the original source should be clearly labeled.

5. What is the basis of the information? In addition to identifying the author(s) of health information, the site should provide citations to the evidence on which the material is based. Opinions or advice should be clearly distinguished from evidence-based information.

6. How is the information selected? Is there an editorial board? Do people with excellent professional and scientific qualifications review the material before it is posted?

7. How current is the information? Websites should be reviewed and updated on a regular basis. It is particularly important that medical information be current. The most recent update or review date should be clearly posted to confirm that the site owners have reviewed the information recently to ensure that it is still valid.

8. How does the site choose links to other sites? Websites usually have a policy about how they establish links to other sites. Some medical sites take a conservative approach and refuse link to any other sites. Some link to any site that requests, or pays, for a link. Others only link to sites that have met certain criteria.

9. What information about the user does the site collect, and why? Websites routinely track the paths visitors take through their sites to determine what pages are being used. However, some health sites ask users to "subscribe" or "become a member." In some cases, this may be so that they can collect a user fee or select information about the user and her or his concerns. In all cases, this will give the site personal information about the user.

    Any credible health site asking for this kind of information should specify what it will and will not do with it. Many commercial sites sell "aggregate" (collected) data about their users to other companies—information such as what percentage of users are women with breast cancer, for example. In some cases, these sites may collect and reuse information that is "personally identifiable," such as zipcode, gender, and birth date. Users should be certain to read and understand any privacy policy or similar language on the site, and know what they are signing up for.

10. How does the site manage interactions with visitors? There should always be a way to contact the site owner for problems, questions, or feedback. If the site hosts chatrooms or other online discussions, it should post the terms for using those services. If the site is moderated who moderates it and why?

Warning Signs and Red Flags

Consumers should be aware that certain words, phrases, and communication techniques tend to signal potentially fraudulent health claims. For example, all of the following should raise suspicions:

- Promises of a miracle cure, new discovery, or satisfaction guaranteed in connection with an alternative treatment.
- Pseudo-medical terms, such as purify, detoxify, energize, often used to impress and cover up a lack of scientific proof.
- Cure-all claims where the manufacturer claims the product treats, cures, or prevents multiple diseases, conditions, or symptoms.
- Anecdotal evidence or testimonials without scientific evidence as support.
- Accusing governmental agencies or the medical profession of suppressing information about a product's benefits.
- Promotion via telephone solicitation, direct mail, or internet.
- Infomercial using talk show format.
- Newspaper ads designed to mimic news articles.

Reporting False or Misleading Health Claims Posted on the Internet

As part of its mission, the FTC investigates complaints about false or misleading health claims posted on the internet. Reports can be made by telephone (1-877-382-4357) or on the FTC website (http://www.ftc.gov/).

Health on the Net Foundation

The HON (accessible at http://www.hon.ch/) is a Swiss foundation that originated at a1995 international conference on the use of the internet in health care. Its mission is to guide health care consumers and providers on the World Wide Web to sound, reliable medical information and expertise. HON provides a highly respected internationally governed and staffed not-for-profit portal to health information on the internet. One of its primary concerns is quality assessment, and toward that end it has developed the HON Code of Conduct for the provision of medical websites. Sites displaying the blue and red HONCode seal have been reviewed by HON and have been found to satisfy its stringent ethical standards for authority, complementarity, confidentiality, attribution, justifiability, transparency of authorship, transparency of sponsorship, honesty in advertising and editorial policy. The HON website also offers visitors a variety of options for targeted searching of sites that have met the requirements of the HON Code of Conduct.

REFERENCES

1. National Center for Complementary and Alternative Medicine. Expanding horizons of health care. Strategic Plan 2005–2009. National Institutes of Health, US DHHS 2005 Washington, DC http://nccam.nih.gov/about/plans/2005/strategicplan.pdf. Accessed June 20, 2006.
2. Barnes PM, Powell-Griner E, McFann K, Nahin RL. Complementary and alterative medicine use among adults: United States, 2002. Advance data from vital and health statistics; no 343. Hyattsville, MD: National Center for Health Statistics. 2004. DHHS Publication No. (PHS) 2004-1250 04-03420 (05/04)
3. Eisenberg DM, Kessler RC, Foster C, Norlock FE, Calkins DR, Delbanco TL. Unconventional medicine in the United States. Prevalence, costs, and patterns of use. N Engl J Med 1993;328: 246–252.
4. White House Commission on Complementary and Alternative Medicine Policy. Final Report. National Institutes of Health, US DHHS 2002 Washington, DC. http://www.whccamp.hhs.gov/pdfs/fr2002_document.pdf. Accessed on June 20, 2006.
5. Institute of Medicine Committee on the Use of Complementary and Alternative Medicine by the American Public. Complementary and Alternative Medicine Use in the United States. Washington DC. The National Academies Press; 2005.
6. Kaptchuk TJ, Eisenberg DM. Varieties of healing. 2: A taxonomy of unconventional healing practices. Ann Intern Med 2001;135: 196–204.
7. Eisenberg DM. Advising patients who seek alternative medical therapies. Ann Intern Med.1997;127:61–69.

8. White J. Alternative sports medicine. The Phys & Sports Med 1998;26 www.physsportsmed.com/issues/1998/06june/white. htm. Accessed on January 16, 2005.

9. Eisenberg DM, Kessler RC, Van Rompay MI, et al. Perceptions about complementary therapies relative to conventional therapies among adults who use both: results from a national survey. Ann Intern Med 2001;135:344–351.

10. Committee on Children with Disabilities. Counseling families who choose CAM for their children with chronic illness or disability. A policy statement of the American Academy of Pediatrics. Pediatrics 2001;107:598–601.

11. Pagan JA, Pauly MA. Access to conventional medical care and the use of complementary and alternative medicine. Hlth Affairs 2005;24:255–262.

12. http://ask.census.gov/cgi_bin/askcensuscfg/php/enduser/ std_alp.php. Accessed on January 30, 2005.

13. Portyanski E. Alternative medicine: how bountiful is the harvest: Drug Topics April 6, 1998:44–50.

14. Chavis LM. Pharmacy-based consulting on dietary supplements. J Am Pharm Assoc 2001;4:181–191.

15. Dietary Supplement Health and Education Act of 1994, Pub L No. 103.417.

16. National Library of Medicine. Consumer health information: a workshop for librarians providing health information to the public. September 1, 2001. http://www.nnlm.gov/train/chi/sws.html

17. Pettigrew AC, King MO, McGee K, Rudolph C. Complementary therapy use by women's health clinic clients. Altern Ther Health Med 2004;10:50–55.

18. Institute of Medicine Committee on the Use of Complementary and Alternative Medicine by the American Public. Complementary and Alternative Medicine Use in the United States. Washington DC. The National Academies Press; 2005.

19. Morris CA, Avorn J. Internet marketing of herbal products. JAMA 2003;290:1505–1509.

20. U.S. General Accounting Office. Health products for seniors. "Anti-aging" products pose potential for physical and economic harm. Report to Chairman, Special Committee on Aging, U.S. Senate. September 2001. GAO-01-1129. Available at http://

ods.od.nih.gov.pubs/gao-01-1129.pdf. Accessed on February 21, 2005.

21. Federal Trade Commission. Promotions for kids dietary supplements leave sour taste. Consumer Feature May 2000. US Federal Trade Commission. www.ftc.gov/bcp/conline/features/kidsupp. htm. Accessed on June 20, 2006.

22. National Library of Medicine. Consumer health information. A workshop for librarians providing health information for the public. DHHS, National Institutes of Health. Bethesda, MD. 2004. www.nnlm.gov/train/chi/sws.htlm. Accessed on January 20, 2005.

23. Neuburger E. Home computer and internet use in the US. August 2000. Special Studies. 2001 US Census Bureau, US Dept. of Commerce. Washington DC. www.census.gov/prod/2001pubs/ p23-207.pdf. Accessed January 30, 2005.

24. Fox S, Rainie L. Vital decisions. How internet users decide what information to trust when they or their loved ones are sick. Washington DC; Pew Internet & American Life Project 2002. www.pewinternet.org/pdfs/PIP_Vital_Decisions_May2002.pdf. Accessed on January 30, 2005.

25. Kaiser Family Foundation. E-Health and the elderly: how seniors use the Internet for health – survey. The Henry J. Kaiser Family Foundation Program for the Study of Entertainment Media and Health. www.kkf.org/entmedia/entmedia011205pkg.cfm. Accessed on January 12, 2005.

26. Bureau of Consumer Protection. Health claims on the Internet: buyer beware. FTC Consumer Feature June 2001. U.S. Federal Trade Commission.

27. Taylor DA. Botanical supplements: weeding out the health risks. Environ Health Perspect 2004;112:A750–A753.

28. Fontanarosa PB, Rennie D, DeAngelis CD. The need for regulation of dietary supplements—lessons from ephedra. JAMA 2003;289:1568–1570.

29. Office of Inspector General, Department of Health and Human Services. Adverse event reporting for dietary supplements: an inadequate safety valve. April 2001. Available at: http:// oig.hhs.gov/oei/reports/oei-01-00-00180.pdf. Accessed on November 30, 2004.

30. Federal Trade Commission. FTC cracks down on marketers of bogus bioterrorism defense products. News Release November 19, 2001. U.S. Federal Trade Commission. http://www.ftc.gov/opa/2001/11/webwarn.htm, Accessed on February 10, 2005.
31. National Association of School Nurses. Position statement: alternative medicine use in the school setting. June 2001. Available at http://www.nasn.org/positions/altermedi.htm. Accessed on January 16. 2005.
32. Beales JH. Statement of the Federal Trade Commission on Efforts to ensure the truthfulness and accuracy of marketing of dietary supplements for children. Before the Subcommittee on Oversight and Investigation, Committee on Energy and Commerce, U.S. House of Representatives. June 6, 2004. Available at http://www.ftc.gov.opa/2004/06/kidsupp.htm Accessed on January 8, 2005.
33. Ambrose PJ. Drug use in sports: a veritable arena for pharmacists. J Am Pharm Assoc 2004;44:501–516.
34. Food and Drug Administration. Press Release: HSS launches crackdown on products containing andro. FDA warns manufacturers to stop distributing such products. March 11, 2004. Available at http://www.fda.gov/bbs/topics/news/2004/hhs_031104.html. Accessed on February 10, 2005.
35. Dasgupta A. Review of abnormal laboratory test results and toxic effects due to use of herbal medicines. Am J Clin Pathol 2003;120:127–137.
36. Fleming MO, Sierpina VS. Ethics Forum: treatment choice is ultimately the patient's. When patients tell of alternative therapies, what do you say? Amer Med News Oct. 4 2004:13.
37. Gabriel B. To teach or not to teach: the role of alternative medicine in the medical school curricula. AAMC Reporter. July 2001. Available at http://ww.aamc.org/newsroom/reporter/july01/alternativemedicine.htm Accessed on September 9, 2004.
38. Wetzel MS, Kaptchuck TJ, Haramati A, Eisenberg D. Complementary and alternative medical therapies: implications for medical education. Ann Intern Med 2003;138:191–196.
39. Neff S. Complementary and alternative medical education. Letter to the Editor. Ann Intern Med 2004;140:67.
40. Fortin AH, Barnett KG. Medical school curricula in spirituality and medicine. JAMA 2004;291:2883.

41. Brokaw JJ, Tunnicliff G, Raess BU, Saxon DW. The teaching of complementary and alternative medicine in U.S. medical schools: a survey of course directors. Acad Med 2002;77:876–881.

42. National Center for Complementary and Alternative Medicine, About the National Center for Complementary and Alternative Medicine. Available at http://nccam.nih.gov/about/aboutnccam/index.htm#2. Accessed on February 18, 2005.

43. CAM Education Grant University of Washington School of Medicine Department of Family Medicine. Available at http://www.fammed.washington.edu/predoctoral/cam/CAM_Grant.html. Accessed on February 18, 2005.

44. Oregon Health and Science University. Grant totaling $1.5 million brings alternative medicine collaboration to OHSU students. News Release. Portland OR. July 30, 2002. Available at http://www.ohsu.edu/news/archive/2002/073002award.html. Accessed on February 18, 2005.

45. Georgetown University Medical Center School Of Medicine. CAM in the curriculum. Educational initiative in CAM. Available at http://som.georgetown.edu/cam/cam_education.htm. Accessed on February 18, 2005.

46. AMSA CAM Initiative American Medical Student Association. Available at http://www.amsa.org/humed/CAM/summary.cfm. Accessed on February 18, 2005.

47. University of Arizona Integrative Medicine Program. Available at http://integrativemedicine.arizona.edu/. Accessed on February 28, 2005.

48. University of Arizona Integrative Medicine Program. Available at http://integrativemedicine.arizona.edu/online_courses/. Accessed on February 28, 2005.

49. University of New Mexico Health Sciences Center Section of Integrative Medicine (SIM) – Education. Available at http://www.unm/medicine/integrative_med/education.shtml. Accessed April 25, 2005.

50. Sierpina VS. Teaching integratively: how the next generation of doctors will practice. Integ Cancer Therapies 2004;3:201–207.

51. Harvard Medical School Osher Institute, Integrative and Complementary Care Mission. Available at http://www.osher.hms.harvard.edu/c_icc.asp. Accessed on March 1, 2005.

52. Whelan JS, Dvorkan L. HolisticKids.org—Evolution of information resources in pediatric complementary and alternative medicine projects: from monographs to Web learning. J Med Libr Assoc 2003;91:411–417.

53. Kemper KJ, Highfield ES, McLellan M, Ott MJ, Dvorkin L, Whelan JS. Pediatric faculty development in integrative medicine. Altern Ther Health Med 2002;8:70–73.

54. Available at http://www.holistickids.org/. Accessed on March 4, 2005.

55. Kligler B, Gordon, A, Stuart M, Sierpina V. Suggested curriculum guidelines on complementary and alternative medicine: recommendations of the Society of Teachers of Family Medicine Group on Alternative Medicine. Fam Med 1999;31:31–33.

56. Institute of Medicine. (IOM) Health professions education: A bridge to quality. Washington DC: The National Academies Press, 2003.

57. Kligler B, Maizes V, Schacter S, et al. Core competencies in integrative medicine for medical school curricula: a proposal. Acad Med 2004;79:521–531.

58. Frenkel M, Ben Arye E. The growing need to teach about complementary and alternative medicine: questions and challenges. Acad Med 2001;76:251–254.

59. Available at http://utmb.edu/cam_edu_education_series.asp. Accessed on March 7, 2005.

60. Health Summit Working Group. Criteria for assessing the quality of health information on the internet – Policy paper. Mitreteck Systems. 1999. http://hifiweb.mitretek.org/docs/policy. Accessed on February 18, 2005.

61. Available at http://nccam.nih.gov/health/webresources/. Accessed on March 17, 2005.

6

Legal and Risk Management Issues in Complementary and Alternative Medicne

Michael H. Cohen, JD, MBA

INTRODUCTION

The integration of complementary and alternative medical (CAM) therapies such as acupuncture and Traditional Chinese Medicine, chiropractic, herbal medicine, massage therapy, and "mind—body" therapies into conventional health care raises important legal and risk management issues for physicians. These include day-to-day questions about how to respond to patient requests for CAM therapies, especially when clinicians disagree with patients on the safety and effectiveness of such care, or when potential adverse interactions with conventional medication are not known or well understood.

Guidance in these matters is not plentiful *(1)*, leaving individual health care providers feeling uncertain as to the best way to respond, and often feeling trapped between a desire to

From: *Biomedical Ethics Reviews: Complementary and Alternative Medicine: Ethics, the Patient, and the Physician*
Edited by: L. Snyder © Humana Press Inc., Totowa, NJ

accommodate the patient's sincere request and the ethical obligation to do no harm. Negotiating this position while maintaining the patient–physician relationship is not easy *(2)*. This chapter addresses several major liability, risk management, and other legal concerns in an attempt to offer some guidance.

APPLICABLE LAW

The provision of CAM care is generally governed by health law and regulations, just as is the case with conventional medical care. But although the principles are largely the same across therapies, there can be more variability in their applicability to CAM providers and therapies. There are also a number of unknowns. The following interlocking areas are key:

1. Licensure
2. Scope of practice
3. Malpractice liability
4. Professional discipline
5. The patient's right of access to treatments
6. Third-party reimbursement
7. Fraud *(3)*.

Each of these areas is briefly described here.

Licensure

Licensure is the requirement that health care providers maintain a current state license to practice their professional healing art. Although a few states recently have enacted statutes authorizing nonlicensed, CAM providers to practice in some circumstances *(4)*, in most states, licensure serves as the first hurdle to professional practice for any health care provider. Licensure of CAM practitioners and the type of license granted varies by state; chiropractors, for example, are licensed in every state, massage therapists and acupuncturists are licensed in more than 50% the states, and naturopaths, in about 12 states *(5)*.

Scope of Practice

The scope of practice refers to the legally authorized boundaries of care within the profession. State licensing statutes usually define a CAM provider's scope of practice; regulations by the relevant state licensing board (e.g., the board of chiropractic or acupuncture) often supplement or interpret the relevant licensing statute. Both statutes and administrative regulations receive interpretation from courts, although they are sometimes construed narrowly *(3)*. For example, chiropractors can give nutritional advice in some states but not in others; and typically, massage therapists are prohibited from mental health counseling.

Physicians, on the other hand, have a broad scope of practice (one that historically has been conceptualized as "unlimited," compared with the limited scope of practice for nonphysicians), as long as the care provided is safe and effective and meets the profession's prevailing standards. If a physician, however, were to provide CAM care such as acupuncture, he or she would, in most states, need to be appropriately trained and credentialed, and providing care that meets medical standards for acupuncture.

In this way, licensure, scope of practice, and also credentialing of health care providers can also serve as factors in considerations of malpractice liability. Because there is variability in the licensing and CAM practitioners across states, and questions about standards of evidence for CAM therapies, some professional liability questions are raised for the CAM practitioner, and for those clinicians who refer or practice jointly with the CAM practitioner.

Malpractice

Malpractice or negligence, is defined as failure to use due care (or to follow the standard of care) in treating a patient with whom there is a relationship, resulting in direct injury to the patient. Generally, each CAM profession is judged by its own standard of care (e.g., acupuncture, chiropractic, physical therapy, massage therapy *[3]*). In cases where the practitioner's clinical care overlaps with medical care (e.g., the chiropractor who takes and reads a patient x-ray) the medical standard may be applied *(3)*.

Malpractice insurance is available for CAM practitioners It should be noted, however, that states vary in their requirements for malpractice coverage *(6)*. The individual practitioner is advised to determine the coverage available and the amount, if any, required by his or her state.

Professional Discipline

Professional discipline is the power of the relevant professional board—for physicians, the state medical board—to sanction a clinician. The most severe sanction is revocation of the clinician's license. Some consumer groups have been concerned about inappropriate discipline, based on what they see as medical board antipathy to the inclusion of CAM therapies in health care. Consumer groups and some physicians in many states therefore have lobbied for "health freedom" statutes—laws providing that physicians may not be disciplined solely on the basis of incorporating CAM modalities into their practice *(3)*. More recently, the Federation of State Medical Boards has issued *Model Guidelines for the Use of Complementary and Alternative Therapies in Medical Practice*, reaffirming this same principle *(7)* (reprinted here as an appendix).

Patient's Right of Access to Treatments

Access to treatments refers to the interest by patients in obtaining therapeutic substances outside typical clinical delivery. These generally fall into two categories: dietary supplements and drugs not approved by the federal Food and Drug Administration (FDA) *(3)*. The former category dominates, as the Dietary Supplement Health and Education Act of 1994 (DSHEA) provided that dietary supplements containing vitamins, minerals, amino acids, and herbs generally were to be regulated as foods, not drugs, and therefore could be sold in interstate commerce without prior proof of safety or efficacy. Since the enactment of the DSHEA, case reports have emerged in the medical literature concerning safety issues associated with various herbal products; studies have shown the possibility for serious adverse herb–drug interactions; and the efficacy of popular supplements such as St. John's Wort has been called into question.

Third-Party Reimbursement

Individual health insurers vary in their coverage of CAM therapies. Third-party reimbursement involves insurance policy provisions, and corresponding legal rules, designed to ensure that reimbursement is limited to "medically necessary" treatment; does not, in general, cover "experimental" treatments; and does not constitute fraud and abuse *(3)*. In general, insurers have been slow to offer CAM therapies as core benefits—largely because of insufficient evidence of safety, efficacy, and cost-effectiveness—although a number of insurers have offered policyholders discounted access to a network of CAM providers.

Health Care Fraud

Health care fraud can come into play in CAM therapies because of the need to prevent intentional deception of patients. Overbroad claims sometimes can lead to charges of fraud, and of misrepresentation, a related legal theory *(3)*.

Fraud and misrepresentation involve the knowing inducement of reliance on inaccurate or false information for the benefit of the person committing the fraud and to the detriment of the victim. The practitioner must know the information or representation is false, or must recklessly fail to discover its falsity, and the victim must reasonably rely on the representation.

A fraud claim typically opens the defending practitioner to the possibility of punitive damages. Fraud is harder to prove than negligence because it requires proving a mental state (intention or recklessness) and not simply that the standard of care was not met. Nonetheless, fraud serves as potent tool to curb overreaching and abusive conduct in provision of CAM therapies. And, allegations of fraudulent conduct also can serve as grounds for claims of negligence (malpractice) and/or professional discipline.

If the clinician or institution submits a reimbursement claim for care that the clinician knew or should have known was medically unnecessary, this also might be grounds for a finding of fraud and abuse under federal law *(3)*.

FOCUS ON MALPRACTICE

This chapter focuses on malpractice liability for use of CAM therapies by physicians. Malpractice liability for CAM practitioners follows similar principles, although standards of care are specific to a health care profession whether conventional or CAM (e.g., physical therapy, medicine, chiropractic, acupuncture).

For physicians, malpractice concerns around CAM therapies are thorny, especially because the research for such therapies is less extensive than for many conventional modalities. Indeed, because the research base is smaller than it is for conventional care, conclusions seem to swing rapidly as new discoveries respectively enhance or diminish validation (e.g., consider the controversy around such therapies as St. John's Wort to treat moderate depression). Yet, as suggested, general principles can be extrapolated from malpractice involving conventional care, because theoretically the same legal concepts and standards should apply, whether the therapy is considered conventional or CAM *(8)*.

One can also apply ethics principles to evaluate the appropriateness of offering or providing CAM therapies. Adams and colleagues offer seven factors to consider in assessing the ethics of whether or not to offer the patient CAM therapies *(9)*:

1. Severity and acuteness of illness.
2. Curability with conventional treatment.

3. Invasiveness, toxicities, and side effects of conventional treatment.
4. Quality of evidence of safety and efficacy of the CAM treatment.
5. Degree of understanding of the risks and benefits of conventional and CAM treatments by the patient.
6. Knowing and voluntary acceptance of those risks by the patient.
7. Persistence of patient's intention to utilize CAM treatment.

Thus, if the illness is not severe or acute, and not curable with conventional treatment, and/or the conventional treatment is invasive and carries toxicities or side effects that are unacceptable to the patient, then, assuming the CAM therapy is not proven unsafe or ineffective, it may be ethically appropriate to try the CAM approach for a limited period of time, while monitoring conventionally. A legal analysis would support this approach as well, especially if the patient fully understands the risks and benefits, is willing to assume the risk of trying such an approach, and insists on this route. In this case, a monitored, wait-and-see approach respects the patient's autonomy interest, while satisfying the clinician's obligation to do no harm.

Grounds for Malpractice

A finding of negligence or medical malpractice generally requires that the following:

1. There was a duty to provide a particular standard of care.
2. The care provided was below the accepted professional standards.
3. There was harm to the patient caused by the physician's failure to meet the professional standard.
4. The patient's injury is one for which there are damages.

Medical experts are retained to testify to standards of care, and the plaintiff's experts will testify that the defendant physician practiced below generally accepted standards of care.

Given this definition, there are multiple possible malpractice claims, including misdiagnosis, failure to treat, failure of informed consent, and fraud and misrepresentation *(10)*. The main sources of concern are probably misdiagnosis and failure to treat because of overreliance on a CAM diagnosis or treatment plan.

Misdiagnosis is the failure to diagnose a condition accurately, or at all. In a misdiagnosis case, a provider who failed to employ conventional diagnostic methods, or who substituted CAM diagnostic methods for conventional ones, risks a malpractice claim.

Adding complementary diagnostic systems (such as those of chiropractic and acupuncture) is not inherently problematic, so long as the conventional bases are covered *(11)*. For example, it would be legally risky to have treated headaches as subluxations or displaced *chi* if the patient turns out to have a brain tumor *(10)*. Continuation of conventional monitoring may be useful in avoiding this type of liability risk *(10,11)*.

Failure to treat with conventional care also can lead to malpractice liability if the patient is thereby injured. Again, it is not the use of CAM therapies per se that is problematic but rather overreliance on such therapies, to the exclusion of necessary medical care. Following the earlier example, if a chiropractor continued to treat headaches without referring the patient to a medical doctor to rule out the possibility of a neurological or cancerous condition, this could constitute failure to treat (or more specifically for the chiropractor, failure to refer to a medical doctor *[10,11]*).

To determine whether using CAM therapies might lead to a liability claim, it is helpful for clinicians to review the medical evidence regarding safety and efficacy for any CAM therapies included in the patient's therapeutic regimen *(11)*. Consider the following framework. Clinicians should evaluate whether the medical evidence (a) supports both safety and efficacy; (b) supports safety, but evidence regarding efficacy is inconclusive; (c) supports efficacy, but evidence regarding safety is inconclusive; or (d) indicates either serious risk or inefficacy *(11)*.

In this scheme, if the medical evidence supports both safety and efficacy, liability is unlikely, and clinicians should recommend the CAM therapy. On the other hand, if the medical evidence indicates either serious risk or inefficacy, a liability claim is probable if harm results, and clinicians should avoid and actively discourage the patient from using the CAM therapy. This is because a therapy that is likely to create harm is probably below acceptable standards of care, and likely to lead to liability claims.

The more difficult considerations are the middle two. If the medical evidence supports safety, but evidence regarding efficacy is inconclusive, or supports efficacy, but evidence regarding safety is inconclusive, then clinicians should caution the patient and, while accepting the patient's choice to try the CAM therapy, continue to monitor efficacy and safety respectively *(11)*. In either case, liability is conceivable but, in most cases, probably unlikely, particularly in the case where the product or service is presumably safe *(11)*. By definition, a therapy that is either safe or effective is unlikely to lead to a liability claim. If, however, the patient's condition deteriorates in either of these two cases, then the physician should consider implementing a conventional intervention, or risk potential liability if the patient becomes injured through reliance on the CAM therapy *(11)*.

Consider, for example, that there is some evidence of safety and efficacy (at this date) for example, for use of chiropractic to treat low-back pain or acupuncture for osteoarthritis of the knee. On the other hand, there is poor evidence regarding use of St. John's Wort to treat severe depression. A clinician who relies on herbal formulas in such a case may risk liability if the patient's condition worsens.

As suggested, if a condition readily can be cured or helped by conventional care, there is a strong legal and ethical imperative to provide such care. Delay in itself is not negligence, however, delay that aggravates the patient's condition or leads to irreversible progression of the disease might be considered as such *(11)*.

On the other hand, engaging the patient in a conversation about options, and suggesting or agreeing to a trial run with a CAM therapy that may have some evidence of safety and/or efficacy in the medical literature, while continuing to monitor conventionally, is a legitimate approach. In this case, the clinician can always intervene conventionally if the CAM therapy turns out to be either unsafe or ineffective.

What happens if the patient has not discontinued conventional therapy, but rather, there is concern about potential complication from the interaction of conventional therapy with the CAM therapy, and there is little, if any, medical literature to inform the clinician (e.g., concerning the combination of a dietary supplement and a prescription drug)?

The liability framework presented earlier presents a good guide for the clinician. Unless there is evidence of a potential adverse interaction, the CAM therapy could be tried while the physician continues to monitor conventionally *(11)*. If the CAM therapy turns out to be either unsafe or ineffective in combination with the conventional therapy, then the clinician accordingly should advise the patient to discontinue use of the CAM therapy *(11)*. Because research regarding CAM therapies is ongoing and the medical evidence can change rapidly, the clinician should communicate regularly with the patient regarding any new developments and reconsider therapeutic decisions accordingly. Integrative care suggests the need for enhanced communications and full patient understanding. Although the legal obligation of informed consent mandates disclosure of risks and benefits (*see* next section), the premise of integrative care goes further in emphasizing the importance of engaging patients in shared decision making.

INFORMED CONSENT

Informed consent law originally was based on the intentional tort of battery, the unauthorized touching of a person. Today, however, almost all jurisdictions view an informed consent claim as a matter of negligence—the failure of the physician to meet the requisite standard to disclose necessary information to the patient. To give informed consent to treatment, the patient must understand his or her condition, the benefits and risks of the proposed treatment, alternative treatments and their benefits and risks, and the prognosis with or without treatment.

Informed consent doctrine goes beyond whether consent was given, to analyze the content and the process of consent. The physician's legal obligation is to provide the patient with all the information material to a treatment decision—in other words, that would make a difference in the patient's choice to undergo or forgo care. This obligation applies across the board, whether CAM or conventional therapies are involved *(12)*. Material information is information about risks and benefits that is reasonably significant to a patient's decision to undergo or forgo a particular therapy. About half the states judge materiality by the "reasonable patient's" notion of what is significant, whereas the other half judge materiality by the "reasonable physician" *(12)*. The principle of shared decision making takes informed consent a step further, by ensuring that there are not only disclosures by physicians to patients, but also full conversations in which patients who wish to be feel empowered and participatory.

Typically, informed consent claims have resulted when a patient is injured by treatment and the treatment itself was not negligent, however, but for the lack of disclosure, he or she would not have undergone the treatment. So, returning to the negligence definition given earlier, to make an informed consent claim in negligence, the patient would need to show that (a) there was a duty to disclose specific information, (b) there was no or inadequate disclosure by the physician, (c) he or she would not have had the treatment had there been adequate disclosure, and (d) there is an injury for which there are damages.

The rise of CAM therapies, however, may lead to new types of claims in which the patient takes issue with no or inadequate disclosure about CAM options. An interesting question is how the law might treat clinicians who fail to make recommendations for patients regarding nutrition, mind–body, and other readily accepted CAM therapies as adjuncts to conventional care. As medical evidence begins to show safety and effectiveness for such therapies, and these therapies become more generally accepted within the medical community, there may be liability for clinicians who fail to make appropriate adjunctive recommendations involving CAM therapies *(3)*. Such a case would likely turn on the court's view of whether the medical profession generally accepted the CAM therapy as safe and effective for the patient's condition, and possibly, as a safer and more effective therapeutic option than the conventional drug or treatment otherwise prescribed *(3)*.

Because of changes in the field, updating the patient about changes in medical evidence regarding CAM therapies may become an important part of informed consent. In any event, informing the patient about the changing medical evidence may shift (in one direction or another) the patient's willingness to accept the known risks and benefits of the CAM therapy, or even to use this therapy, and thus is material to the patient's decision. This is especially important as more information emerges about adverse effects of various therapies. It can also, however, be challenging, as many patients equate what has been promoted to them as "natural" care—especially regarding herbal products—with "safe" care. As part of informed consent and shared decision making, the physician should actively strive to correct such a misperception.

Referrals and Vicarious Liability

A major concern in the realm of malpractice involves the potential liability exposure for physician referrals to a CAM practitioner. Although there are few judicial opinions setting precedent regarding referrals to CAM therapists, the general rule in conventional care is that there is no liability merely for referring to a specialist. There is no particular reason why this rule should not be applied to any referral, whether for conventional or CAM care.

One of the exceptions to this general rule, however, involves "joint treatment," in which various clinicians collaborate to develop a treatment plan and to monitor and treat the patient. Such coordinated care is a premise of integrative care. It suggests that liabilities may be shared within the integrative care team; for example, between the psychiatrist and the acupuncturist. Ensuring that referred-to providers have competence and a good track record in their area of expertise will help reduce potential liability risk.

Another question that frequently arises is whether to refer only to licensed providers. Again, there is no statute or case mandating such a rule, and a lot is left to the risk management tolerance of the individual clinician or institution. And some states, as noted, explicitly authorize nonlicensed practitioners to offer CAM therapies. The theory of licensure is that it ensures some minimal level of competence, although it does not always succeed. And the "joint treatment" exception may be applied whether the CAM provider receiving the referral is licensed or not.

Another exception involves the "known incompetent": if the referral itself was inherently negligent; that is, if the referring provider knew or should have known that the CAM provider was incompetent, then the referring clinician can be held negligent *(8)*. Therefore, the referring clinician should ensure that the CAM provider receiving the referral, whether licensed or not, has the highest level of credentialing (i.e., evidence of education, training, skill, and competence) for that discipline.

Existing Case Law

Few judicial opinions address malpractice and CAM therapies; the legal landscape is relatively new and subject to rapid change as CAM therapies increasingly penetrate mainstream healthcare. The leading malpractice cases are *Charell v. Gonzales (13)* and Schneider v. Revici *(14)*.

In *Charell*, a physician used hair analysis and nutritional care to diagnose and treat a cancer patient. The jury found that the physician had departed from accepted medical practice, which departure caused the patient injury. In denying the physician's motion to set aside the verdict, the court stated that "no practitioner of alternative medicine could prevail ... as ... the term 'nonconventional' may well necessitate a finding that the doctor who practices such medicine deviates from 'accepted' medical standards" *(13)*.

Such a finding, that using a CAM therapy invariably deviates from the standard of care, leaves even physicians who responsibly integrate such therapies into clinical practice with malpractice exposure under this definition. Therapies lacking sufficient support through consensus standards, in other words, would create risk of liability irrespective of any actual lack of due care in selecting or utilizing the CAM treatment.

In *Schneider*, the patient sought nonsurgical treatment for breast cancer. She signed a detailed consent form releasing Dr. Revici from liability. Following the treatment, the tumor spread. The jury found Dr. Revici liable for malpractice but halved the award, finding the patient 50% comparatively negligent. The US Court of Appeals for the Second Circuit, reversing, held that the trial judge should have instructed the jury that express assumption of risk (through the release the patient signed) was a complete defense to the claim of physician malpractice *(14)*.

The court distinguished express assumption of risk (in which the patient agrees in advance that the physician need not follow conventional standards of care, agrees to the use of CAM therapies, and assumes the risks of their use) from implied assumption of risk (which is founded on the patient's reasonable, voluntary, and intelligent consent to the risk of harm from the physician's conduct). Under New York law, express assumption of risk completely exonerates the physician, and "dissolve[s] the physician's duty to treat a patient according to medical community standards"; whereas implied assumption of risk triggers comparative negligence, in which the physician's liability is reduced to the extent of the patient's responsibility or fault.

Dietary Supplements: Especially Problematic

Although legal rules regarding potential malpractice liability are becoming clearer, recommendations involving herbal products remain especially difficult to manage. Under the Dietary Supplement Health Education Act of 1994, "dietary supplements" containing vitamins, minerals, amino acids, and herbs generally are regulated as foods, not drugs, and therefore can be sold in interstate commerce without prior proof of safety or efficacy. Furthermore, the federal Food and Drug Administration rarely interferes with individual clinicians' practices, because it is a federal agency and health care practice is regulated under state law.

Nonetheless, many authorities remain skeptical about the role of supplements in health care generally. The medical literature is full of reports about safety concerns associated with various herbal products. In addition to issues of contamination and adulteration, and lack of batch-to-batch consistency, clinicians have to consider the possibility of adverse herb–herb as well as herb–drug interactions. The literature on efficacy and effectiveness is sparse next to that on comparable pharmaceutical medications for the same conditions.

The sale of dietary supplements from the physician's office is ethically questionable and legally risky. The American Medical Association and the American College of Physicians have said that physician sale of dietary supplements for profit may present an impermissible conflict of interest between good patient care and profit, and are thus ethically objectionable. Several states have enacted laws limiting or prohibiting physician sales of dietary supplements *(15)*.

Yet another concern is potential discipline by the relevant state medical boards. Many of the statutes contain generic provisions that allow physician discipline, for example, for such acts as "failure to maintain minimal standards applicable to the selection or administration of drugs, or failure to employ acceptable scientific methods in the selection of drugs or other modalities for treatment of disease" *(16)*. Some state medical boards in the past have applied these provisions to physicians offering nutritional treatments. For nonphysicians, nutritional care may or may not be part of the clinician's authorized scope of practice.

Risk Management

Good communications between patient and clinician is a hallmark of high-quality care, one that can enhance informed consent practices. It can also be an effective risk management tool. In conventional medicine, many lawsuits stem from the combination of bad outcomes and poor communication with patients, leading to subsequent misunderstanding or anger on the part of patients and families.

Risk management in CAM would also include monitoring for potential adverse reactions between conventional and CAM therapies, such as, for example, adverse herb–drug interactions, particularly when the patient is taking dietary supplements along with medication or undergoing surgery. Certainly, the few CAM legal cases have emphasized the importance of conventional diagnosis and monitoring when CAM therapies are recommended or not discouraged. This is probably the most important means of ensuring that patients do not receive substandard care. Continuing to monitor conventionally, and intervene conventionally when medically necessary, helps assure that the standard of care will have been met, and the possibility of patient injury minimized. For example, the physician and patient may wish to try a CAM therapy for a predefined period of time instead of conventional care (e.g., a combination of herbal products and lifestyle changes) and return to conventional care (prescription medication) when it becomes necessary.

From a liability perspective, the more acute and severe the condition, the more important it would be to monitor and treat conventionally. Again, the definition of medical malpractice emphasizes failure to follow the standard of care, and patient injury. The greater the disease's severity, the more likely patient injury will result from relying too heavily on a CAM therapy—and thus the greater possibility for a lawsuit resulting in malpractice liability. Furthermore, the more curable the condition conventionally, the more likely a court would see failure to provide (or even, perhaps, insist) on such standard care as negligent.

In addition, poor documentation in medical records will not assist a clinician in defending against a claim, and can suggest negligence to a jury. In general, it is advisable to keep complete and accurate medical records that include documentation of the patient's medical history concerning use of CAM therapies, and of conversations with patients concerning potential inclusion of such therapies. Such thorough documentation can help physicians prove that informed consent requirements were satisfied, and also may help protect against undue disciplinary action by state medical boards concerned with use of CAM therapies *(11)*. If the physician recommends or does not discourage use of a CAM therapy based on the medical literature, it is a good idea to keep a file of the medical literature supporting the specific medical recommendation. On the other hand, if the physician believes that, based on the medical literature the patient's continued use of one or more CAM therapies is medically inadvisable, and the patient insists on using such therapies against medical advice, this should be documented in the medical record.

Physicians also should familiarize themselves with documentation standards suggested by the Federation of State Medical Board Guidelines, and whether these are applicable in their state or home institution (*see* the next section). Finally, under the legal doctrine known as "assumption of risk," a defense to medical malpractice is provided where the patient has chosen a therapeutic course despite the physician's efforts to dissuade and discourage this *(17)*. In some states, if patients continue to use a CAM therapy against the physician's advice, and this is documented in the medical record, assumption of risk may be a defense to a malpractice action *(17)*.

Assumption of risk has been allowed as a defense in at least one case involving patient election of a CAM therapy instead of conventional care (i.e., of a nutritional protocol in lieu of conventional oncology care), *Schneider v. Revici*. Some attorneys might advise physicians to have the patient sign a waiver, expressly stating that the patient knowingly and voluntarily chose the CAM therapy or regimen—such as energy healing and a nutritional protocol, instead of the recommended conventional treatment. Courts, however, tend to disfavor waivers of liability in medical malpractice cases, taking the perspective that medical negligence cannot be waived away, and that the physician remains responsible for the patient's treatment. Physicians should, nonetheless, engage in clear conversations with patients concerning options involving CAM therapies, since such an approach respects patient autonomy, helps meet the requirements of informed consent, promotes the ideal of shared decision making, and encourages interactive positive relationships.

Federation of State Medical Board Guidelines

As noted, the Federation has passed model guidelines for: "(1) physicians who use CAM in their practices, and/or (2) those who co-manage patients with licensed or otherwise state-regulated CAM providers" *(7)*. These guidelines offer a framework for individual state medical boards to regulate physicians who integrate CAM therapies into their practices. They should be read in conjunction with existing medical board guidelines in the state in which the physician practices. In general, the guidelines "allow a wide degree of latitude in physicians' exercise of their professional judgment and do not preclude the use of any methods that are reasonably likely to benefit patients without undue risk." The guidelines also recognize that "patients have a right to seek any kind of care for their health problems," and that "a full and frank discussion of the risks and benefits of all medical practices is in the patient's best interest" *(7)*. To this extent, the guidelines implicitly recognize both shared decision making and the interest of patients in integrative care.

At the same time, in trying to assess whether an integrative care practice is appropriate or if it should trigger physician discipline, the guidelines ask the following questions:

- Is the selected therapy *effective and safe?* (Is there adequate scientific evidence of efficacy and/or safety or greater safety than other established treatment models for the same condition?)
- Is the selected therapy *effective, but with some real or potential danger?* (Does it have evidence of efficacy, but also of adverse side effects?)
- Is the selected therapy *inadequately studied, but safe?* (Is there insufficient evidence of clinical efficacy, but reasonable evidence to suggest relative safety?)
- Is the selected therapy *ineffective and dangerous?* (Has it been proven to be ineffective or unsafe through controlled trials or documented evidence or as measured by a risk–benefit assessment?) *(7)*.

Some of these standards may be difficult to meet. For example, the first category is stated in terms of the CAM therapy having greater evidence of safety and/or efficacy than the applicable conventional treatment; there may or may not be available evidence to suggest whether this condition is met. Moreover, the guidelines list these four categories but do not offer suggestions for how to utilize the categories in clinical decision making.

In addition to these standards, the guidelines provide an extensive checklist of items to which the physician must attend when providing CAM therapies. The physician practicing integrative care should review these items with legal counsel and determine which are advisable and practical. For example, these items include documentation regarding the following:

- The medical options that have been discussed, offered, or tried. If they have been discussed, offered, or tried, to what effect? A statement should be included as to whether or not certain options have been refused by the patient or guardian.

- Proper referral has been offered for appropriate treatment.
- The risks and benefits of the use of the recommended treatment to the extent known have been appropriately discussed with the patient or guardian.
- The physician has determined the extent to which the treatment could interfere with any other recommended or ongoing treaWtment *(7)*.

The guidelines also provide that the CAM treatment should be tailored to the individual and evaluated under a documented treatment plan. The treatment should achieve the following:

- It should have a favorable risk–benefit ratio compared with other treatments for the same condition.
- It should be based on a reasonable expectation that it will result in a favorable patient outcome, including preventive practices.
- It should be based on the expectation that a greater benefit will be achieved than that which can be expected with no treatment *(7)*.

The guidelines are suggestive but not binding in any given state, unless adopted by that state's medical board.

CONCLUSION

Guiding patients regarding CAM therapies involves clinical, ethical, and legal considerations, many of which are still evolving. As medical evidence accumulates, practices and standards of care will change, moving forward responsible mechanisms for integrating CAM into conventional care. As CAM therapies become even more prevalent and medicine responds, the legal and regulatory framework for health care practice will evolve, also.

Appendix: Federation of State Medical Boards Model Guidelines for the Use of Complementary and Alternative Therapies in Medical Practice

Approved by the House of Delegates of the Federation of State Medical Boards of the United States, Inc., as policy April 2002.

Introduction

Physicians, indeed all health care professionals, have a duty not only to avoid harm but also a positive duty to do good—that is, to act in the patient's best interest(s). This duty of beneficence takes precedence over any self-interest.[1]

Because of the increasing interest in and use of complementary and alternative therapies in medical practices (CAM), state medical boards have a responsibility to assure that licensees utilize CAM in a manner consistent with safe and responsible medicine. On behalf of the Federation of State Medical Boards and its continued commitment to assist state medical boards in protecting the public and improving the quality of health care in the United States, the Special Committee for the Study of Unconventional Health

Care Practices (Complementary and Alternative Medicine),[2] undertook an initiative in April 2000 to develop model guidelines for state medical boards to use in educating and regulating (1) physicians who use CAM in their practices, and/or (2) those who co-manage patients with licensed or otherwise state regulated CAM providers.

CAM is a fluid concept that has been defined differently by various organizations and groups. For the purposes of these guidelines, the Committee has chosen to use the term CAM as defined by the National Institutes of Health (NIH) National Center for Complementary and Alternative Medicine (NCCAM) (see Definitions). The Committee acknowledges that some therapies deemed CAM today may eventually be recognized as conventional, based on evidence over time.

This initiative focuses on encouraging the medical community to adopt consistent standards, ensuring the public health and safety by facilitating the proper and effective use of both conventional and CAM treatments, while educating physicians on the adequate safeguards needed to assure these services are provided within the bounds of acceptable professional practice. The Committee believes adoption of guidelines based on this model will protect legitimate medical uses of CAM while avoiding unacceptable risk.

The intention of the Committee is to provide guidelines that are clinically responsible and ethically appropriate. These guidelines are designed to be consistent with what state medical boards generally consider to be within the boundaries of professional practice and accepted standard of care.

Model Guidelines for the Use of Complementary and Alternative Therapies in Medical Practice

Section I. Preamble

The (*name of board*) recognizes that the practice of medicine consists of the ethical application of a body of knowledge, principles and methods known as medical science and that these objective standards are the basis of medical licensure for physicians of the state of (*name of state*). These standards allow a wide degree of latitude in physicians' exercise of their professional judgment and do not preclude the use of any methods that are reasonably likely to benefit patients without undue risk. Furthermore, patients have a right to seek any kind of care for their health problems. The Board also recognizes that a full and frank discussion of the risks and benefits of all medical practices is in the patient's best interest.

There are varying degrees of potential patient harm that can result from either conventional medical practices or CAM:

- Economic harm, which results in monetary loss but presents no health hazard;
- Indirect harm, which results in a delay of appropriate treatment, or in unreasonable expectations that discourage patients and their families from accepting and dealing effectively with their medical conditions;
- Direct harm, which results in adverse patient outcome.

Regardless of whether physicians are using conventional treatments or CAM in their practices, they are responsible for practicing good medicine by complying with professional standards and regulatory mandates. In consideration of the above potential harms, the (name of board) will evaluate whether or not a physician is practicing appropriate medicine by considering the following practice criteria. Is the physician using a treatment that is:

- **Effective and safe?** (having adequate scientific evidence of efficacy and/or safety or greater safety than other established treatment models for the same condition)
- **Effective, but with some real or potential danger?** (having evidence of efficacy, but also of adverse side effects)
- **Inadequately studied, but safe?** (having insufficient evidence of clinical efficacy, but reasonable evidence to suggest relative safety)
- **Ineffective and dangerous?** (proven to be ineffective or unsafe through controlled trials or documented evidence or as measured by a risk–benefit assessment)

Inasmuch as the (*name of board*) is obligated under the laws of the state of (*name of state*) to protect the public's health, safety and welfare and recognizes that the standards used in evaluating health care practices should be consistent, whether such practices are regarded as conventional or CAM, the Board recognizes that a licensed physician shall not be found guilty of unprofessional conduct for failure to practice medicine in an acceptable manner solely on the basis of utilizing CAM. Instead, the Board will use the following guidelines to determine whether or not a physician's conduct constitutes a violation of the state's Medical Practice Act.

Section II. Definitions

For the purposes of these guidelines, the following terms are defined as indicated:

COMPLEMENTARY AND ALTERNATIVE THERAPIES IN MEDICAL PRACTICES (CAM)

CAM refers to a broad range of healing philosophies (schools of thought), approaches and therapies that mainstream Western (conventional) medicine does not commonly use, accept, study, understand, or make available. A few of the many CAM practices include the use of acupuncture, herbs, homeopathy, therapeutic massage, and traditional Oriental medicine to promote well-being or treat health conditions.

People use CAM treatments and therapies in a variety of ways. Therapies may be used alone, as an alternative to conventional therapies, or in addition to conventional, mainstream therapies, in what is referred to as a complementary or an integrative approach. Many CAM therapies are called holistic, which generally means they consider the whole person, including physical, mental, emotional and spiritual aspects.[3]

CONVENTIONAL MEDICAL PRACTICES

Conventional medical practices refer to those medical interventions that are taught extensively at US medical schools, generally provided at US hospitals, or meet the requirements of the generally accepted standard of care.

Section III. Guidelines

The *(name of board)* has adopted the following guidelines when evaluating the delivery or co-management of CAM:

EVALUATION OF PATIENT

Parity of evaluation standards should be established for patients whether the physician is using conventional medical practices or CAM.

Prior to offering any recommendations for conventional and/ or CAM treatments, the physician shall conduct an appropriate medical history and physical examination of the patient as well as an appropriate review of the patient's medical records. This evaluation shall include, but not be limited to, conventional methods of diagnosis and may include other methods of diagnosis as long as the methodology utilized for diagnosis is based upon the same standards of safety and reliability as conventional methods, and shall be documented in the patient's medical record. The medical record should also document:

- What medical options have been discussed, offered or tried, and if so, to what effect, or a statement as to whether or not certain options have been refused by the patient or guardian; that proper referral has been offered for appropriate treatment;
- That the risks and benefits of the use of the recommended treatment to the extent known have been appropriately discussed with the patient or guardian;
- That the physician has determined the extent to which the treatment could interfere with any other recommended or ongoing treatment.

TREATMENT PLAN

The physician may offer the patient a conventional and/or CAM treatment pursuant to a documented treatment plan tailored to the individual needs of the patient by which treatment progress or success can be evaluated with stated objectives, such as pain relief and/or improved physical and/or psychosocial function. Such a documented treatment plan shall consider pertinent medical history, previous medical records and physical examination, as well as the need for further testing, consultations, referrals or the use of other treatment modalities.

The treatment offered should:

- Have a favorable risk–benefit ratio compared to other treatments for the same condition;
- Be based on a reasonable expectation that it will result in a favorable patient outcome, including preventive practices;
- Be based on the expectation that a greater benefit will be achieved than that which can be expected with no treatment.

CONSULTATION AND/OR REFERRAL TO LICENSED OR OTHERWISE STATE-REGULATED HEALTH CARE PRACTITIONERS

The physician may refer the patient as necessary for additional evaluation and treatment in order to achieve treatment objectives and may include referral to a licensed or otherwise state-regulated health care practitioner with the requisite training and skills to utilize the CAM therapy being recommended. However, the physician is responsible for monitoring the results and should schedule periodic reviews to ensure progress is being achieved.

DOCUMENTATION OF MEDICAL RECORDS

The physician should keep accurate and complete records to include:

- The medical history and physical examination;
- Diagnostic, therapeutic, and laboratory results;
- Results of evaluations, consultations, and referrals;
- Treatment objectives;
- Discussion of risks and benefits;
- Appropriate informed consent;

- Treatments;
- Medications (including date, type, dosage, and quantity prescribed);
- Instructions and agreements;
- Periodic reviews.

Records should remain current and be maintained in an accessible manner, and readily available for review.

EDUCATION

All physicians must be able to demonstrate a basic understanding of the medical scientific knowledge connected with any method they are offering or using in their medical practices as a result of related education and training.

SALE OF GOODS FROM PHYSICIAN OFFICES

Due to the potential for patient exploitation, physicians should not sell, rent or lease health-related products or engage in exclusive distributorships and/or personal branding;

- Physicians should provide a disclosure statement with the sale of any goods, informing patients of their financial interest; and
- Physicians may distribute products to patients free of charge or at cost in order to make products readily available.
- Exceptions should be made for the sale of durable medical goods essential to the patient's care, as well as nonhealth-related goods associated with a charitable or service organization.[4] [Language on the sale of goods from physician offices is contained in the report of the Special Committee on Professional Conduct and Ethics as adopted in April 2000.]

CLINICAL INVESTIGATIONS

As expected of those physicians using conventional medical practices, physicians providing CAM therapies while engaged in the clinical investigation of new drugs and procedures (a.k.a. medical research, research studies) are obligated to maintain their ethical and professional responsibilities. Investigators shall be expected to conform to the following ethical standards:

- Clinical investigations should be part of a systematic program competently designed, under accepted standards of scientific research, to produce data that are scientifically valid and significant.
- A clinical investigator should demonstrate the same concern and caution for the welfare, safety, and comfort of the patient involved as is required of a physician who is furnishing medical care to a patient independent of any clinical investigation.[5]

Furthermore, investigators shall be expected to abide by all federal guidelines and safeguards, such as approval and monitoring of the clinical trial by an Institutional Review Board (IRB), when applicable, to ensure the risks to the patient are as low as possible and are worth any potential benefits.

In Conclusion

The Committee recognizes that legitimate standards of medical practice are rooted in competent and reliable scientific evidence and experience. However, these standards are subject to continual change and improvement as advances are made in scientific investigation and analysis. In addition, standards of medical practice to some degree, and the provision of medical services in individual circumstances in particular, are influenced by psychological, social, political and market forces. It is the responsibility of state medical boards to balance all of these considerations in fulfilling their mission of protecting the public through the regulation of the practice of medicine.

Public protection is carried out, in part, by ensuring physicians in all practices, whether conventional or CAM, comply with professional, ethical and practice standards and act as responsible agents for their patients. Accordingly, the Federation encourages state medical boards to adopt these guidelines to assist them in educating and regulating physicians who are (1) engaged in a practice environment offering conventional and/or CAM treatments; and/or (2) engaged in cooperative therapeutic relationships for their patients with a nonphysician licensed or otherwise state-regulated health care ractitioner offering CAM.

State medical boards should ensure a balance between the goal of medical practices being evidence-based while remaining compassionate and respectful of the dignity and autonomy of patients. This balance should also ensure informed consent and minimize the potential for harm.

The Federation reaffirms its commitment to cooperate with physicians and professional, governmental and other organizations and agencies in supporting the further study of all health care practices that offer promise.

REFERENCES

AMA. Policy E 2.07: Clinical Investigation.

Eisenberg DM, Kaptchuk TJ. Varieties of healing, 2: a taxonomy of unconventional healing practices. *Annals of Internal Medicine.* August 2001;135:196–208.

Fontanarosa PB, ed. AMA's *Alternative Medicine: An Objective Assessment.* 2000.

FSMB. *Report on Professional Conduct and Ethics.* April 2000. Web version at www.fsmb.org, Policy Documents.

Illinois Department of Professional Regulation Medical Disciplinary Board. *Board Policy Statement: Complementary and Alternative Therapies.* November 1999.

Kentucky Board of Medical Licensure. *Board Policy Statement: Complementary and AlternativeTherapies.* March 1999.

Nevada State Board of Medical Examiners. *Non-Conventional Medical Treatment Regulations.* August 2000;Section 1:Chapter 630.

NIH. General Information About CAM and the NCCAM, Publication M-42 — June 2000, *NCCAM Clearinghouse,* Web version updated

02/21/01

Schneiderman L. Medical ethics and alternative medicine. *The Scientific Review of Alternative Medicine*. Spring/Summer 1998;2(1): 63–66.

Texas State Board of Medical Examiners. *Standards for Physicians Practicing Integrative and Complementary Medicine*. November 1998;Chapter 200.

Special Committee for the Study of Unconventional Health Care Practices (Complementary and Alternative Medicine): 2001–2002

Paul M. Steingard, DO, Chair
Past Board Member
Arizona Board of Osteopathic Examiners in Medicine and Surgery

William L. Harp, MD
Executive Director
Virginia Board of Medical Examiners

Edward S. Hicks, Sr.
Secretary/Treasurer
Texas State Board of Medical Examiners

Elizabeth P. Kanof, MD
President
North Carolina Medical Board

Daniel B. Kimball, Jr., MD
Board Member
Pennsylvania State Board of Medicine

Irvin A. Rothrock, MD
Board Member
Alaska State Medical Board

Ralph W. Stewart, MD
Board Member
Indiana Health Professions Bureau

Maralyn E. Turner, PhD
Board Member
Oregon Board of Medical Examiners

Gary E. Winchester, MD
Board Member
Florida Board of Medicine

Federation Staff

Dale L. Austin, MA
Interim Chief Executive Officer

Bruce A. Levy, MD, JD
Deputy Executive Vice President, Leadership Services

Lisa Robin
Assistant Vice President, Leadership and Legislative Services
Pat McCarty
Administrative Associate, Leadership Services

The Federation thanks the following consultants for their efforts in providing input to these guidelines:

David M. Eisenberg, MD—Bernard Osher Associate Professor of Medicine; Director, Division for Research and Education in Complementary and Integrative Medical Therapies, Harvard Medical School

Russell H. Greenfield, MD—Medical Director, Carolinas Integrative Health, Carolinas HealthCare System; Visiting Assistant Professor, University of Arizona College of Medicine

Kenneth R. Pelletier, PhD, MD (hc)—Chairman, American Health Association; Clinical Professor of Medicine, University of Maryland School of Medicine and University of Arizona School of Medicine

---

[1]Schneiderman L. Medical ethics and alternative medicine. The Scientific Review of Alternative Medicine. Spring/Summer 1998;2,(1):63–66.

[2]In 1995, the Federation established a special committee charged with developing strategies for recommendation to state medical boards for the regulation and discipline of physicians who engage in unsafe and/or deceptive health care practices. The Federation's House of Delegates adopted the Committee's recommendations as policy in April 1997. That same year, the Committee was charged with providing objective information to medical boards for their use in educating licensees, the public and state legislators on issues surrounding health care practices that may be potentially harmful and/or deceptive. In 2000, the Committee was charged with the development of these guidelines.

[3]NIH. General Information About CAM and the NCCAM, Publication M-42—June 2000, NCCAM Clearinghouse, Web version updated 02/21/01

[4]FSMB. Report on Professional Conduct and Ethics. HOD April 2000, Web version at www.fsmb.org, Policy Documents.

[5]AMA. Policy E 2.07: Clinical Investigation.

(Reprinted with permission of the Federation of State Medical Boards of the United States, Inc.,www.fsmb.org)

ACKNOWLEDGMENTS

The underlying legal analysis on which this chapter is based has appeared in a number of forms, including the sources referenced and three earlier, primary texts by the author.

REFERENCES

1. Cohen MH, Ruggie M. Integrating complementary and alternative medical therapies in conventional medical settings: legal quandaries and potential policy models. Cinn L Rev 2004;72:2:671-729.
2. Cohen MH. Negotiating integrative medicine: a framework for provider-patient conversations. Negotiation Journal 2004;30:3; 409-433.

3. Cohen MH. Complementary and Alternative Medicine: Legal Boundaries and Regulatory Perspectives. Baltimore, MD: Johns Hopkins University Press, 1998.
4. Cohen MH. Healing at the borderland of medicine and religion: regulating potential abuse of authority by spiritual healers. J Law & Relig 2004;18(2):373–426.
5. Eisenberg DM, Cohen MH, Hrbek A, Grayzel J, van Rompay MI, Cooper, RA. Credentialing complementary and alternative medical providers. Ann Intern Med 2002;137:965–973.
6. American Medical Association. Liability Insurance Requirements. Available at http://www.ama-assn.org/ama/pub/category/print/4544.html Accessed March 9, 2004.
7. Federation of State Medical Boards, Model Guidelines for Use of Complementary and Alternative Therapies in Medical Practice. Available at www.fsmb.org.,Accessed February 5, 2005.
8. Studdert DM, Eisenberg DM, Miller FH, Curto DA, Kaptchuk TJ, Brennan TA.
Medical malpractice implications of alternative medicine. JAMA 1998;280:1610–1615.
9. Adams KE, Cohen MH, Jonsen AR, Eisenberg DM. Ethical considerations of complementary and alternative medical therapies in conventional medical settings. Ann Intern Med 2002;137:660–664.
10. Schouten, R, Cohen MH. Legal issues in integration of complementary therapies into cardiology. In: Frishman WH, Weintraub MI, Micozzi MS, eds. Complementary and Integrative Therapies for Cardiovascular Disease. New York: Elsevier, 2004, pp.
11. Cohen MH, Eisenberg DM. Potential physician malpractice liability associated with complementary/integrative medical therapies. Ann Intern Med 2002;136:596–603.
12. Ernst EE, Cohen MH. Informed consent in complementary and alternative medicine. Arch Intern Med 2001;161(19):2288–2292.
13. *Charell v. Gonzales*. 660 NY (Supp. II) 665, 668 (S.Ct., NY County 1997), affirmed and modified to vacate punitive damages award, 673 NY (Supp. II) 685 (App. Div., 1st Dept. 1998), reargument denied, appeal denied, 1998 NY App. Div. LEXIS 10711 (App. Div., 1st Dept. 1998), appeal denied, 706 Northea. Rprtr. 2d 1211 (1998).

14. *Schneider v. Revici*. 817 F.2d 987 (2d Cir. 1987).
15. Dumoff, A. Medical Board Prohibitions Against Physician Supplements Sales, Alternative/Complementary Therapies 2000;6(4):226–236.
16. Ohio Rev. Code Ann. § 4731.22 (18).
17. Cohen MH. Beyond Complementary Medicine: Legal and Ethical Perspectives on Health Care and Human Evolution. Ann Arbor: University of Michigan Press, 2000.

7

Whose Evidence, Which Methods?

Ethical Challenges in Complementary and Alternative Medicine Research

Jon Tilburt, MD, MPH

INTRODUCTION:
CAM, Diversity, and the Ethics
of Clinical Research

This chapter provides an overview of ethical issues in research on complementary and alternative medicine (CAM). Such a discussion must include commonly accepted ethical concepts from research ethics combined with an understanding of some specific features of CAM research and practice. This chapter adopts the definitions of CAM used by the National Center for Complementary and Alternative Medicine (NCCAM) at the National Institutes of Health (Table 1 *[1]*).

From: *Biomedical Ethics Reviews: Complementary and Alternative Medicine: Ethics, the Patient, and the Physician*
Edited by: L. Snyder © Humana Press Inc., Totowa, NJ

Table 1
Definitions of Complementary and Alternative Medicine (CAM)
and Conventional Medicine

CAM

CAM, as defined by the National Center for Complementary and Alternative Medicine, is a group of diverse medical and health care systems, practices, and products that are not presently considered to be part of conventional medicine.

Conventional medicine

Conventional medicine is medicine as practiced by holders of medical doctor or doctor of osteopathy degrees and by their allied health professionals, such as physical therapists, psychologists, and registered nurses. Other terms for conventional medicine include allopathy; Western, mainstream, orthodox, and regular medicine; and biomedicine. Some conventional medical practitioners are also practitioners of CAM.

From ref. *1*.

The Context of CAM Research

There has always been a great degree of diversity in healing approaches within and across cultures. In recent decades, there has been resurgence in public attention paid to diverse health practices. This resurgence has been correlated with shifts in the social authority of conventional medicine, greater awareness of healing approaches from other cultures to which the public has greater exposure (e.g., China), and changes in how knowledge and expertise are defined by the public *(2)*. Patients often are drawn to CAM practices because of dissatisfaction with conventional care, for wellness, or for greater congruence with their philosophical orientation to life *(3)*.

Within the broad category of CAM, particular CAM systems explain symptoms differently. For instance, in ayurvedic medicine (called *Ayurveda*) a symptom like back pain could be explained as a disruption of energy flow from one of many energy centers called *chakrahs*. That same pain could be understood in chiropractic as a spinal misalignment, called *subluxation*. Such differences in vocabulary and diagnostic constructions are closely related to treatment paradigms. Similarly, many healing practices have their own logic and way of interpreting information that may differ significantly from those of conventional medicine. Each CAM healing approach may have a different way of applying knowledge. In conventional medicine, clinical expertise, patient preference, and the literature from clinical trials are said to form the basis for decision making *(4)*. Although this broad framework may work for many CAM approaches, others may rely on practical experience, opinions of colleagues, and theoretical models of how the body works in making treatment decisions. Patients, too, may find appealing aspects of either an evidence-based approach or a more experience-based approach depending on their own philosophical orientation, the nature of the condition, or their trust in the profession *(3)* or individual practitioners.

As patient demand for and use of CAM have become increasingly common, it has become important to scientifically evaluate various CAM practices, and objectively characterize their benefit or harm in scientific terms. This approach of applying the methods of clinical research to CAM is important in meeting basic information needs of the public, medical professionals, and third-party payers regarding popular products and services. Growing interest in CAM research culminated in 1998 when the US Congress authorized the establishment of the NCCAM at the NIH. In the midst of this growing attention to research on various CAM therapies, ethical principles must be applied.

Ethical Principles for Biomedical Research

Ethical principles of biomedical research have been articulated for contemporary biomedicine in the Belmont Report *(5)*. One commonly accepted set of ethical principles that arose out of the Belmont Report has been further refined by Beauchamp and Childress in their landmark work, *The Principles of Biomedical Ethics (6)*. These principles include nonmaleficence, beneficence, respect for autonomy, and justice. Rooted in common aspects of morality across different times and cultures, these principles are an attempt to unify diverse values and preferences without necessarily settling age-old disagreements between different ethical theories (e.g., utilitarian vs deontological theories) and conflicting cultural norms.

The practical beauty of the principles is that they have wide appeal and support in the medical community and serve as a good starting point for ethical deliberation. However, applying these principles often requires further refinement in order for them to practically guide actions and to resolve conflicts among the principles *(7)*.

Emanuel and colleagues have synthesized seven requirements drawn from several authoritative bodies in a comprehensive and practical framework for determining what makes research ethical *(8)*. These elements include social value, scientific validity, fair subject selection, favorable risk–benefit ratio, independent review, informed consent, and respect for participants. These elements make ethical ideals (including the principles outlined earlier) more practical when applied to actual research studies.

Ethical Challenges of Studying CAM in an Age of "Plural Medicine"

Some have argued that most healing traditions including conventional medicine have distinct worldviews. The term *worldview* describes the philosophical life perspective of an individual or group that is central to how that person or group goes about living *(9)*. Differences in worldviews about health may limit the degree to which meaningful communication and understanding can occur across healing disciplines, challenge professional relations, and make ethical deliberations difficult, particularly with respect to CAM and CAM research.

Given such disagreement, one might wonder whether a principle-based approach is feasible or appropriate for the ethics of CAM research. Because many CAM approaches are based on different philosophical assumptions, why can we be confident bioethical principles apply to CAM at all? Despite the initial intuitive appeal of this concern, there are important common ethical themes across healing practices that suggest that a basic ethical congruence exists among various CAM and conventional healing settings. These common themes include a healing relationship, an interest in the patient's well-being, and the desire to get well. These common experiential elements of all healing traditions are an important starting point that justifies a principles approach to CAM research ethics.

Although the principles outlined by Beauchamp and Childress do arise from common elements from across a variety of healing traditions, they do not explicitly address the moral significance of these diverse approaches to healing. Instead, their framework was formulated in an era where the dominance of conventional medicine was unquestioned. This raises questions regarding how to best apply ethical principles in a world in which multiple medicines co-exist and interact.

Moreover, conducting socially valuable, scientifically valid research on various CAM therapies raises additional questions about what it means to conduct ethical research. Can conventional scientific methods and standards be applied to alternative practices? Do current research methods provide an unbiased description of CAM practices and outcomes from CAM interventions? Must one assume the worldview of the CAM therapeutic system in order to appropriately study the healing practices of that system? Faced with these questions, CAM researchers must constantly both affirm and respect the cultures and beliefs out of which CAM practices arise while also recognizing their need to produce credible and practical science. Despite the importance of ethical reflection on issues in CAM research, little has been written in the medical literature addressing ethical issues specific to CAM research *(10)*.

After first reviewing an ethical framework proposed by a recent Institute of Medicine (IOM) report on CAM, this chapter provides an overview of the most salient ethical issues at stake in modern CAM research initiatives. The chapter concludes with some challenges faced in integrating CAM research evidence into clinical practice.

THE PRINCIPLES MEET PLURAL MEDICINE: AN ETHICAL FRAMEWORK FROM THE IOM

In 2005, the IOM published a report entitled, *Complementary and Alternative Medicine in the United States (11)*. This comprehensive report serves as an overview of CAM as it exists in the United States, including a chapter dedicated to ethical issues entitled, "An Ethical Framework for CAM Research, Practice, and Policy." Here we summarize and briefly comment on the "Value Commitments" presented by the IOM report including questions raised by those commitments.

The ethical framework for CAM as articulated in the IOM report includes five value commitments:

1. A social commitment to public welfare.
2. A commitment to protect patients.
3. A respect for patient autonomy.
4. Recognition of medical pluralism.
5. Public accountability.

Public Welfare

The good of patients and the public is a key to the ethics of most healing practices and is therefore important for analyzing the ethics of CAM research as well. Public welfare implies the obligation of health practitioners and public health officials to hold the well-being of patients and populations in the highest regard, and is consistent with the principle of beneficence.

Safety

The commitment to protect patients from hazardous medical practices is the second value commitment. In the research arena, this commitment implies the need to better characterize and communicate the safety profile of CAM therapies. This is consistent with the principle of nonmaleficence. One important area where safety research would benefit the public is in herbal medicines. Herbal medicines are one of the most common forms of biologically based CAM therapies used in the United States. The importance of such research became evident in recent years as reports of potential herb–drug interactions (e.g., St. John's Wort) and herbal adulteration (e.g., heavy metals in some ayurvedic herbs) became more widely known. Research to further characterize the safety profile of these products would enhance the ethical commitment to safety outlined by the IOM ethical framework *(12)*.

Autonomy

The IOM report articulates respect for patient autonomy as the third value commitment in the chapter on the ethics of CAM. Although autonomy may not be viewed similarly across different worldviews *(13)*, the validity of the concept is equally important for CAM research and practice in modern society, including the ethical requirement of informed consent *(14,15)*.

Medical Pluralism

Medical pluralism is the fourth value commitment in the IOM report and represents the most significant conceptual addition to a principles approach to the ethics of CAM. Because of this, it is discussed in more detail. Although the exact meaning of *medical pluralism* is not well defined in the ethics literature, the IOM report borrows this concept from medical anthropology and sociology literature as a way of sensitizing the reader to special ethical concerns related to the co-existence of plural healing practices *(16)*. The IOM report says that this involves an "acknowledgment of multiple valid modes of healing, and a pluralistic foundation for health care." Because there is such a range of healing approaches that co-exist in modern society, ethical decision-making processes must acknowledge and accommodate this reality. With respect to research the basic concern is that conventional and CAM approaches to accumulating knowledge may begin with very different starting points about what constitutes knowledge, what standards of evidence are used to evaluate new observations, and what background information is deemed important in designing research. Unless they recognize these different starting points, researchers may assume that their own way of studying healing techniques is the best or only way to study a therapeutic approach. Medical pluralism suggests that such a perspective may be too narrow or limiting.

Thus, the obligations of medical pluralism at a minimum include acknowledgment of differences in knowledge assumptions, methods of testing ideas, and criteria for determining whether an observation is a confirmation or refutation of the tested idea. Medical pluralism in short means a "commitment to openness." When applied to CAM research, the IOM report states the following:

> Investigation of CAM practices entails a moral commitment of openness to diverse interpretations of health and healing, a commitment to finding innovative ways of obtaining evidence, and an expansion of the knowledge base relevant and appropriate to medical practice. This commitment to openness also includes reconsideration of the meaning and the relevance of ethical norms that guide various research and clinical activities. *(11)*

From this discussion we can presume at least two senses of medical pluralism as a concept—a factual sense and a moral sense.

The factual sense of medical pluralism as a concept would mean that diversity is a fact of life in modern health care, and diversity in healing practices is part of the overall diversity. This can be known from observations such as those of Eisenberg and colleagues *(17)*. The moral sense of medical pluralism accepts the factual nature of multiple healing approaches and adds to that certain ethical obligations. This moral sense of medical pluralism implies that we should go beyond acknowledgment and actually act differently because there are so many potential approaches to healing. According to the IOM, just recognizing the facts is not sufficient, but rather medical pluralism requires a "moral commitment of openness."

The nature and extent of those obligations to openness, however, are not clear from the IOM report. At the very least, this moral sense of medical pluralism would find something inherently worthy of respect in the differences so apparent in plural medicines. Medical pluralism would recognize that conventional medicine has its own culture *(18)*, entails a posture of tolerance toward those who are different from the medical establishment, and ascribes legitimacy to the other party despite this difference.

Along with tolerance, many would continue the logic of the moral pluralist to argue that those in the medical profession need to exercise some degree of caution in making judgments about healing paradigms outside the biomedical model of health and disease—a kind of professional humility. This is consistent with a growing awareness of and interest in the ethical aspects of cultural competency and patient-centered care *(19)*.

Particularly important for this chapter, the report goes on to discuss implications of medical pluralism for how research is conducted. Quoting Howard Brody, the IOM report states the following:

> Therapies that might be highly effective within the proper
> cultural and belief context might prove to be totally inef-

fective within the foreign environment required for and
created by the conduct of an RCT [randomized controlled
trial]. *(11)*

This quote implies that the moral obligations related to medical
pluralism extend to research methods.

Many serious questions remain about the meaning and
significance of medical pluralism, especially as it relates to the
other ethical principles. Is it a fifth principle with the same status
and importance as autonomy, nonmaleficence, beneficence, and
justice? Is it a rule that helps us better apply the four principles?
Does openness and willingness to engage other healing traditions
imply scientific skepticism about the possibility of knowledge
using existing scientific methods? Does a belief in diverse health
beliefs commit one to bioethical relativism, where one cannot
make universally valid judgments about the rightness and wrong-
ness of an action in research or practice? These issues go beyond
the scope of this chapter but need to be explored elsewhere in
order for medical pluralism to work well as a value commitment
in the ethics of CAM.

Public Accountability

The final value commitment stated in the IOM report is public
accountability. This value commitment relates directly to the
responsibilities that accompany public funding for health care
and biomedical research. Public accountability ensures that
those entrusted with public resources are held accountable to
utilize those resources with prudence and fairness. Public accountability implies an obligation not just to account for and respect the
diverse interests but also to exercise the practical judgment to
balance competing interests with prudence and fairness in service of the public trust given researchers. In this sense, public
accountability is analogous to the principle of justice outlined by
Beauchamp and Childress *(6)*. Justice is the principle that insists
that risks and benefits be distributed fairly and that preference

not be given to someone solely on the basis of their social status. In the case of CAM research, prudent, equitable judgments must be made that balance interests of organizations, whole populations, and society.

Although most of the value commitments in this report are closely aligned with basic bioethical principles, future scholarship needs to explore how these value commitments relate to one another, and how potential conflicts between these value commitments can be resolved. For instance, how should officials who are responsible for distributing public funds balance and account for medical pluralism in weighing the merits of funding proposals that examine Reiki, a form of spiritual and energy therapy, the scientific basis for which is not well described? Should such research be given less priority because of it may be less likely to benefit society given our current state of knowledge? Or should we admit there might be limitations in the ability of the scientific method to study it? Or, in light of medical pluralism, should such research be given greater priority, recognizing that such research may help science overcome its current limitations in knowledge and may advance its methodology? This is just one example of the challenges that will be faced in applying these value commitments in arena of science policy.

Using this framework, one can see that applying the principles to CAM is possible, but the process of application may be more difficult where presuppositions about the meaning of health, science, and knowledge conflict. This is particularly true in the process of research oversight and priority setting that will require accounting for both medical pluralism and public accountability.

In summary, the value commitments enumerated by the IOM report on CAM fit within the general framework set out by Beauchamp and Childress, but with a heightened attention to the realities of plural health practices that co-exist in contemporary society. With this conceptual background we can now explore a few of the most common ethical issues in CAM research. The following section outlines how the value commitments articulated by the IOM may help identify and address challenging ethical aspects of CAM research, while at the same time it outlines some questions that persist even with this framework.

APPLYING ETHICAL PRINCIPLES IN CAM RESEARCH: WHAT TO STUDY, AND HOW TO STUDY IT

Complex ethical questions in CAM research arise across the whole spectrum of the research process starting from deciding what to study, determining how to study it, and determining what outcomes to study. A controversial research report on a treatment from Traditional Chinese Medicine (TCM), *moxibustion*, illustrates potential ethical value judgments involved early on in deciding what to study. Several authors have discussed this case in a recent book edited by Callahan *(20)*.

Little is known in the biomedical literature about the mechanisms by which moxibustion may work. "Moxibustion is a traditional Chinese method that uses the heat generated by burning herbal preparations containing *Artemisia vulgaris* (mugwort) to stimulate acupuncture points" (a mechanism that makes no sense in a Western biomedical paradigm) and was tested in a clinical trial for correction of breech position in pregnancy. Results suggested statistically significant positive effects on fetal positioning at the time of birth *(21)*.

This study caused controversy in the medical literature. CAM advocates praised this potentially benign intervention, whereas conventional skeptics were disturbed by the study's implications. On ethical grounds, each argued for or against moxibustion as a legitimate, ethical topic for a research study. CAM advocates said there is a moral duty to explore better alternatives to changing fetal position than are currently used in obstetric practice, as fetal position affects morbidity and mortality of delivery. Conversely, skeptics were appalled that such a study ever got approval from an Institutional Review Board, because there was "clearly" no "biologic plausibility" to the study's hypothesis *(22)*. These skeptics said that unless there is an underlying biological mechanism (within the Western scientific framework) in which to make sense of these results, similar future research should not go forward because it is not a legitimate area in which the risks and benefits of research are likely to favor subject participation.

Additional questions that arise in the process of determining what to study include questions about definitions. CAM has been defined in different ways by different stakeholders *(23–25)*, with *CAM* being a convenient label that those in conventional medicine place on "others" to describe everything "not them." Although seemingly innocuous, even the label *CAM* itself can reveal a value judgment about the healing approach including meanings like unscientific, unproven, or primitive. After deciding on a definition of CAM or a particular CAM treatment, researchers then must answer two very basic questions: First, is CAM worth studying, especially with public funds? Second, if so, what research questions about CAM merit investigation?

The first consideration involves determining whether CAM is worth studying. Some authors have argued that CAM is not worth studying because it is fundamentally unscientific and quackery *(26,27)*. However, the prevalent use of CAM by the public is strong reason to suggest that further investigation of CAM may be necessary to meet beneficence and nonmaleficence obligations. If some CAM treatments are at least marginally beneficial, a regard for public welfare (beneficence) compels further research. If some CAM therapies are harmful, it is important for research to document that harm. Therefore, based on these ethical principles, many CAM therapies are ethically worthy of investigation using public funding.

The second question concerns which scientific questions merit investigation. As alluded to earlier, questions addressing the safety of commonly used self-administered treatments would be important to study as would studies testing the safety and efficacy of treatments for common conditions for which there are limited conventional options (e.g., low back pain).

Ethical issues also arise in answering the questions, "What is a promising treatment to study?" and "When is it appropriate to begin studying that treatment in human populations?" These questions are important in all of research but may be more challenging to answer in CAM research. For example, in conventional drug development, candidate formulations are studied on the molecular and cellular level prior to being tested in animals. Then, when promising effects are found in animals, and basic safety parameters are clarified, investigators may pursue a standard process of investigating new drugs and devices often under federal regulatory oversight. Only through this rigorous process can a treatment get to the point of being studied in humans. This process attempts to assure public accountability and nonmaleficence with the eventual goal of benefit (beneficence) for the public.

These questions about deciding what treatments are worth studying pose a particular problem in CAM research because of the way many CAM therapies have come into use. For instance, most herbal products have not been developed and introduced into popular use in such a linear fashion. Instead, over time, popular use and historical precedent have been relied on as determinants of usefulness. Under these circumstances, investigators and policymakers are faced with a decision about whether the information currently available warrants further investigation as a treatment.

If there is no in vitro evidence or animal models do not exist to document safety and promise of efficacy, are investigators justified in studying an herb in the general population? If so, under what circumstance are such decisions justifiable? Moreover, does historical precedent of human use provide adequate grounds for pursuing study in human populations? These are some of the questions faced by those overseeing CAM studies. These questions bring to bear several ethical considerations including welfare (beneficence), safety (nonmaleficence), medical pluralism, and public accountability. One example of how this process plays out is in a recent NIH policy requiring prior dosing and standardization data before conducting efficacy trials of herbal medicines *(28)*. Given a scientific commitment to credible science and the need to be able to fairly interpret the meaning of study results for herbal medicines, federal research administrators implemented these measures that must precede large-scale trials of herbal medicines, as an attempt to optimize the value of herbal medicine research and maintain public accountability in the research administration process.

This example demonstrates the tension in balancing public accountability and medical pluralism in research planning. Public accountability requires that the public not invest in studies of "quackery" *(29)* and that scientifically reliable and clinically useful information results from research. Medical pluralism requires that scientists and reviewers be careful in deciding too quickly what is "quackery." Medical pluralism argues against scientific dogmatism about biological plausibility; rather investigators may need to keep an open mind about what is biologically plausible.

Once it has been determined that something may be worth studying, further value judgments go into defining the research question. This includes judgments in defining the condition for which that agent will be tested, and the criteria established to define that condition.

For instance, milk thistle (*Silybum marianum*), is a common herb used to treat mild disorders of the liver. It was first used for biliary conditions in the first century AD and since then has been popular in Europe and the United States as well as by practitioners of Chinese herbal medicine for treatment of various liver conditions *(30)*. Its efficacy is not well established, but it is considered by herbalists to be safe in a range of conditions. One question for the researcher interested in studying this herb includes how to define the clinical condition in which to study milk

thistle. Will the researcher define the clinical condition of interest in allopathic terms, like "biliary colic," or will the researcher
instead define the condition of interest based on a particular
"CAM" tradition's classification system like "liver qi stagnation"
from TCM, or "carrying of bile" for which it was originally used?

The choice of what condition to study involves value judgments with profound scientific and ethical implications. A conventional classification, like "hepatitis" or biliary colic would
help one understand how milk thistle might be applied in conventional contexts. A TCM classification, like "stagnation of liver
qi" may help us better understand efficacy as applied in the context of a CAM medical system, but may limit its usefulness in
more conventional settings. Applying medical pluralism for these
definitional issues will involve balancing the relative merits of
selecting one or both the classification approaches in order to
produce science that is socially valuable and scientifically valid.

Bell et al. suggested study design innovations that test the
efficacy of particular healing modalities based on both allopathic
and CAM-system related classification schemes *(31)*.

> Western [conventional] medical research usually assumes
> that its approach to diagnosis is the preferred way to label a
> patient. It requires homogeneous groups of patients with
> conventional diagnoses for study. But each system of CAM
> has its own theory-driven method for categorizing patients.
> Within a group of patients with asthma, for example, each
> CAM system is likely to identify several different subtypes.
> . . .For homogeneity of study samples, ideal designs would
> involve a double selection procedure: first, for a specific
> conventional diagnosis, and second, for a specific CAM sys-
> tem diagnosis.. . . *(31)*

Such an approach, although complex and potentially costly,
would constitute a pluralistic approach to research design, and
may have the greater user utility when the evidence is finally produced because its results could be interpreted in either conventional or CAM system terms. Conversely, failure to appreciate

the effects of these definitions many lead to inappropriate acceptance or rejection of certain modalities based on biases in the way
the research question is framed rather than on the actual effects of
the agent tested. Such a pluralistic approach may be difficult and
would require further exploration. As a matter of practical rel-
evance, emphasizing CAM research on conditions or symptoms
that can be readily understood in both conventional and CAM
terms could increase the social value of CAM research. For
instance, the symptoms known in conventional medicine as
gastroesphageal reflux disease have analogous classification in
TCM related to excesses in spleen qi that make them potentially
more amenable to CAM research.

Ethical Issues in Study Design

Ethical challenges related to study design are problems not
unique to CAM research, *per se*, but may be especially apparent
in CAM. In addition to the issues discussed previously—describing the treatment, defining the condition of interest, and determining a "promising" therapy for study—decisions must be made
regarding which scientifically rigorous design is best to answer
the question of interest.

In general, once safety and preliminary evidence of clinical
usefulness are established, clinical research to definitively determine safety and efficacy is designed to measure the difference in
outcomes between at least two groups with different exposures. In
order to ensure that research results are valid, researchers take
pains to define and measure all known important potential variables that may influence the outcome of interest and "control for"
those variables that might influence the outcome. If this does not
occur, users of the evidence will not be able to distinguish causal
associations from confounding associations *(32)*. This is a general
challenge in clinical research that is not unique to CAM research.

In the modern era, the randomized controlled trial (RCT) has
become the scientific gold standard in clinical research design.
A brief examination of ethical questions related to the RCT

design, the ethical requirement for equipoise, and the placebo effect will illustrate some of the ethical challenges that arise in deciding how to study CAM therapies.

Ethical Challenges for Randomized Controlled Trials

The RCT is a research design approach that randomly allocates selected research participants to a treatment group or a control group. This approach enables investigators to distinguish between outcome differences that may be due to chance or natural history vs outcome differences than can be attributed to the study treatment. This approach minimizes bias and maximizes cause–effect determination. Because of these practical benefits, RCT is now an indispensable scientific tool and is the method of choice internationally to measure the causal effects of new treatments in a manner that minimizes bias. This evolution of the RCT was a critically important practical innovation in modern biomedical science *(33)*.

General criticisms of this design approach include concerns about internal vs external validity. A primary objective of RCTs is to establish internal validity by proving "efficacy" of a treatment. "Efficacy" describes the effects attributable to a specific intervention in a controlled experiment. External validity means the degree to which a study's results are applicable to general populations. Positive outcome measures that are externally valid in clinical research are referred to as measures of "effectiveness." Effectiveness refers to the effects attributable to a specific intervention when applied in a population that more closely resembles populations seen in clinical practice. The emphasis placed on establishing efficacy in RCTs, so it is argued, does not answer the real questions practitioners have regarding effectiveness. Achieving a balance between internally valid research that tests for efficacy (with randomized designs, strict inclusion/exclusion criteria, blinding, etc.) and more externally valid research that tests effectiveness in real clinical practice settings is a general challenge for all clinical research that seeks to have social value. These criticisms have prompted many in conventional medicine to call for more practical approaches to testing interventions in the real world *(34)*. This has led some to revisit the utility of different study designs such as observational and qualitative studies *(35)*.

There are also specific concerns about the use of the RCT design in research on CAM. First, CAM advocates have claimed that testing for a single causal relationship, as RCTs tend to do, defies the inherent complexity that many CAM healing traditions assume *(31)*. In some of these complex CAM traditions, the whole treatment intervention is purportedly greater than the sum of its parts, and individual components of an intervention cannot be isolated from synergistic accompanying treatment components. To test one component of a complex healing modality, it is argued, does not answer an important question from within that CAM perspective. (This criticism may be less important, for instance, in research on individual herbal medicines, whose use and treatment are very analogous to medication prescribing. In such cases, an RCT design should work as well as it does for conventional drugs.)

These ethical, practical challenges amplify when decisions are made on how best to fairly study CAM *whole medical systems* originating from other cultures. "Whole medical systems are built upon complete systems of theory and practice. Often, these systems have evolved apart from and earlier than the conventional medical approach used in the United States."[1] Designing a realistic clinical trial of a whole medical system that incorporates the characteristic cultural and symbolic features of that system may not be possible, or may be exceeding costly. For instance, if one wanted to study the medicinal effects of acupuncture for nausea, is it enough to demonstrate the relative efficacy or inefficacy of acupuncture as compared to a standard anti-emetic in a cancer center? Or must we study the intervention in China, as a component of a holistic way of healing in order to make judgments regarding its efficacy? The particular scientific concern made clearer by the concept of medical pluralism is that a study isolated from its holistic context that shows a negative result (i.e. inefficacy) may not be actual proof of no treatment benefit unless it is studied in context.

In light of these general and CAM-specific concerns about RCTs, the IOM ethical framework sheds light on how these concerns can be addressed. Medical pluralism suggests that researchers must remain open to the possibility that not all CAM approaches are subject to scientific evaluation, or if they are, certain design accommodations may be necessary to accurately test for the effects of a CAM treatment. On the other hand, public accountability demands that in prudence and fairness, CAM and conventional treatments should be subject to the same basic scientific standards. For instance, public accountability would be poorly served by a wholesale abandonment of RCTs *(36,37)*. In addition to echoing some of the general RCT criticisms discussed here, the IOM proposes some potential methodological and analytic accommodations specific to CAM, including *N*-of-1 trials and preference RCTs *(12)*.

An *N*-of-1 trial approach is an experimental technique that allows an individual patient to be treated with the intervention in a blinded fashion intermittently over a given time period, half of the time with the treatment and half with the control. Results from individual trials could then be pooled for aggregate analyses. Then participants would be compared to themselves from times when they were treated vs times they received controls. Preference RCTs are trials that allow patients to choose the arm of the study they would like to be treated in, introducing an element of self-selection into the research design. This more accurately mimics real healthcare seeking behavior, but introduces selection bias. Although not a definitive solution to complex methodology questions, such design accommodations represent the kind of methodological openness called for by the IOM.

Ethical Requirement of Equipoise

A second area of ethical concern in using RCTs for CAM research involves the ethical requirement of equipoise. Equipoise is a state of genuine uncertainty about the efficacy of a particular intervention. The ethical requirement for equipoise in research is based on the importance of a favorable risk–benefit ratio for participants deriving from ethical principles of nonmaleficence and beneficence. Some have argued that without equipoise on the part of investigators, RCTs cannot be ethically conducted *(38)*. For example, it would not be ethical to conduct a RCT of β-blockers and calcium channel blockers for post-myocardial infarction care, because there is not equipoise on this issue in biomedicine and therefore the risk–benefit ratio for participation by current standards of knowledge would be unfavorable.

General ethical questions about the equipoise requirement include questions about to whom the requirement applies. Is it to the researcher, to the patient's doctor, or to the broader research community? One common formulation states that equipoise should refer to the current state of the evidence or the current standard of care. These questions are still debated in the ethics literature.

When applied specifically to CAM research, some have raised a concern that equipoise could not be achieved for many researchers who deliver CAM interventions in a clinical trial. It is argued that by their very nature many CAM therapies, such as Reiki, require and incorporate the clinician's expectations and beliefs into the treatments themselves. Because of this requirement to believe in the therapy, an RCT would not be ethically acceptable because equipoise cannot be achieved. Either the researcher would be promoting (in his or her view) an unfavorable risk–benefit ratio to the control group, or the researcher would fail to deliver an authentic form of the therapy.

Although these concerns are understandable, there is reason to believe that for all research equipoise must be achieved not for the individual researcher or practitioner involved in research, but by the research community. If this is true, an RCT of Reiki would still be an acceptable design because equipoise is possible even when the provider believes strongly in its benefits. In the spirit of medical pluralism CAM research can ethically accommodate the strong belief in the efficacy of the treatment, while maintaining a fair and prudent assessment of efficacy that public accountability requires.

Ethical Aspects of Placebo Controls

Ethical concerns surrounding the placebo effect, the use of placebo controls, and measurement of the placebo response are common in CAM research. The placebo effect is the change in a patient's clinical condition attributable to the patient's expectations. Although some have challenged its existence *(39),* there is a growing body of evidence, suggesting it is real, and elucidating specific mechanisms by which it might operate *(40).* Usually, investigators are interested in ascertaining the specific effects of investigational treatments and use a placebo control group to measure effects that might come from expectations of patients, as well as the body's self-healing, the natural history of disease, or changes owing to interactions with research staff. In clinical research, these changes are considered together as the *placebo response*, but should be distinguished from the placebo effect seen in clinical practice *(41).* Placebo controls in clinical research are typically thought of as biologically inert substances or procedures administered in clinical trials that look, taste, smell, or feel like the active intervention (e.g. "sugar pills," sham acupuncture).

General concerns about placebos include value-based assumptions about the importance of the placebo effect by physicians and researchers as well as the ethical use of placebo controls in clinical trials. Physicians commonly consider placebo effects as nuisance factors in both medical practice and in the results of clinical research. However, it may be important to consider the potential value of the placebo effect, especially for conditions in which there are no other proven treatment options. Physicians in these circumstances may be more interested in the magnitude of the effects or the centrality of a healing relationship rather than the specificity of the mechanism by which those effects came about *(42–44)*. Researchers must also consider the placebo effect. For instance, it may be important to estimate the expected placebo response rate to a given intervention in order to appropriately plan sample sizes in designing a study. In both cases, there may be implicit or explicit value judgments that what is *really important* are the specific effects of interventions other than the placebo control. These value judgments arise from ethical assumptions.

Although it can be argued that the use of placebos in clinical practice is a form of deception that is not routinely warranted because it violates the principle of beneficence, placebo use under conditions of valid informed consent in the context of research are not necessarily problematic. Ethical arguments favoring placebo use in clinical trials include the moral obligation to produce the most credible evidence possible for or against putative experimental interventions.

These questions about the meaning of the placebo effect and the importance of placebo controls extend to specific concerns related to obligations in CAM research design. Miller and colleagues address issues of randomized placebo controlled trials and their importance for CAM research. They conclude that public health and safety mandate the same ethical requirements for all clinical research and that the RCT with placebo controls should be use for assessing the efficacy of CAM treatments whenever feasible and ethically justifiable.

The placebo effect may be a primary mechanism by which the purported benefits of some CAM therapies are mediated *(44)*. This raises the possibility that in order for researchers to meet their ethical obligations to identify beneficial treatments, they may also need to measure placebo effect as primary treatment end points measured against no-treatment controls. While modern biomedicine typically regards treatments that are no better than placebo as therapeutically worthless, medical pluralism placebo responses that have demonstrated superiority to no-treatment controls can be viewed as efficacious in their own right even if the mechanism of their benefit is primary mediated by patient expectations and neuron-humeral responses to those expectations. In this sense, medical pluralism as applied to study design, may stretch a researcher's conception of benefit in an open-minded and pragmatic way.

Ethical Challenges in Interpretation/Application of CAM Research Evidence

The preceding discussion of ethical issues in research design leads us to a more general set of concerns regarding the ethical challenges of interpreting and applying the results of clinical research in CAM. This chiefly concerns how the users of clinical research findings most ethically apply the limited data they do have regarding CAM. Especially because evidence regarding CAM is still limited, there is considerable uncertainty regarding how this data might apply in clinical practice. Like most clinical research, the populations in which particular interventions are studied do not always resemble the patients seen commonly in primary care settings, and the studies themselves have various limitations that create uncertainty about their meaning for clinical practice. This problem of applying population-based research results to specific practice settings is a general problem in achieving evidence-based practice. Thus, the ethical challenge to the clinician is how to interpret and apply the research that does exist in a way that promotes the well-being of patients, is alert to safety concerns, while maintaining integrity and ethical values as a professional.

The process of interpreting and applying research evidence inevitably incorporates subjective and objective components. As the field of clinical research has evolved, theorists have become increasingly aware of the various forms of bias that can play into evidence interpretation. The interpretations of clinical trial results are probabilistic statements that must be interpreted in light of other existing knowledge.

The ethical challenge in interpretation is to try to understand new data on both CAM and conventional treatments with both skepticism toward entirely new observations (for which there may be little theoretical basis) and openness to the possibility that existing theory may not be sufficient. This is easier said than done. In reality interpretation of any results usually invokes one or more types of interpretive bias *(45)*. Researchers interested in promoting knowledge should acknowledge the limitation of their approach to evidence interpretation. This process should recognize that biases exist, and should strive to be transparent about those biases in applying the evidence. If these improvements to evidence interpretation from clinical research could be achieved throughout the biomedical world, they could then lead to a more balanced, thoughtful, and pragmatic approach to interpreting the results of CAM research (because the issues for interpreting research on CAM and conventional treatments are essentially the same). Especially in a world of plural medicines, interpreters of the research evidence in CAM owe it to their patients to be transparent about their biases and transparent about the gaps in their knowledge when discussing the state of the research evidence either as part of clinical care or as part of informed consent in CAM research. These issues are discussed at length in earlier chapters.

The ethical interpretation and application of CAM research evidence will require a greater awareness of CAM research, a greater willingness to accept the findings of that research, and a greater ability and willingness on the part of conventional and CAM practitioners to apply the evidence from research to clinical practice. In an age of plural medicines, physicians at a minimum must be prepared to counsel patients about risks and benefits of common self-administered therapies like dietary supplements (e.g., know common herb–drug interactions), be able to advise patients about ineffective therapies, and be open to recommending treatments with sound evidence of safety and efficacy *(45)*. By taking a critical, but patient-centered approach under conditions of uncertainty, physicians can better meet the needs of their patients *(46)*.

CONCLUSION

CAM research poses many ethical challenges to researchers and clinicians trying to use such research evidence. Practitioners and researchers should appreciate and accommodate diverse health perspectives while preferentially recommending therapeutic options for which reliable evidence suggest a favorable risk–benefit ratio. This requires a greater awareness of assumptions in diverse healing approaches. With such awareness, researchers and practitioners will be better equipped to apply sound ethical principles while accommodating the diverse health preferences of those they serve in their research and clinical practice.

REFERENCES

1. NCCAM (National Center for Complementary and Alternative Medicine). Online. http://nccam.nih.gov/health/whatiscam/. Accessed March 8, 2006.
2. Kaptchuk TJ, Eisenberg DM. Varieties of healing. 1: medical pluralism in the United States. Ann Intern Med 2001;135(3):189–195.
3. Astin JA. Why patients use alternative medicine: results of a national study. JAMA 1998;279(19):1548–1553.
4. Haynes RB, Devereaux PJ, Guyatt GH. Clinical expertise in the era of evidence-based medicine and patient choice. ACP Journal Club 2002;136:A11

5. United States, National Commission for the Protection of Human Subjects of Biomedical and Behavioral Research. The Belmont report: ethical principles and guidelines for the protection of human subjects of research : appendix. no. (OS) 78-13–78-14 ed. Washington, DC: Dept. of Health, Education, and Welfare, National Commission for the Protection of Human Subjects of Biomedical and Behavioral Research, 1978.
6. Beauchamp TL, Childress JF. Principles of biomedical ethics, 5th ed. Oxford: Oxford University Press, 2001.
7. Richardson HS. Specifying, balancing, and interpreting bioethical principles. J Med Philos 2000; 25(3):285–307.
8. Emanuel EJ, Wendler D, Grady C. What makes clinical research ethical? JAMA 2000; 283(20):2701–2711.
9. Nicholi AM. Definitional and significance of a worldview. In: Josephson AM, Peteet JR eds. Handbook of Spirituality and Worldview in Clinical Practice. Washington, DC: American Psychiatric Publishing, 2003.
10. Miller FG, Emanuel EJ, Rosenstein DL, Straus SE. Ethical issues concerning research in complementary and alternative medicine. JAMA 2004;291(5):599–604.
11. IOM (Institute of Medicine). Complementary and Alternative Medicine in the United States. Washington, DC:National Academies Press, 2005.
12. IOM (Institute of Medicine). Dietary Supplements: A Framework for Evaluating Safety. Washington, DC: National Academies Press, 2004.
13. Carrese JA, Rhodes LA. Western bioethics on the Navajo reservation. Benefit or harm? JAMA 1995;274(10):826–829.
14. Faden RR, Beauchamp TL, King NMP. A History and Theory of Informed Consent. New York: Oxford University Press, 1986.
15. Sugarman J. Informed consent, shared decision-making, and complementary and alternative medicine. J Law Med Ethics 2003;31(2):247–250.
16. Leslie C. Medical pluralism in world perspective. Soc Sci Med [Med Anthropol] 1980;14B(4):191–195.
17. Eisenberg DM, Kessler RC, Foster C, Norlock FE, Calkins DR, Delbanco TL. Unconventional medicine in the United States. Prevalence, costs, and patterns of use. N Engl J Med 1993;328(4):

246–252.

18. Taylor JS. Confronting "culture" in medicine's "culture of no culture." Acad Med 2003;78(6):555–559.
19. Paasche-Orlow M. The ethics of cultural competence. Acad Med 2004;79(4):347–350.
20. Callahan D. The Role of Complementary and Alternative Medicine: Accommodating Pluralism. Washington, DC: Georgetown University Press, 2002.
21. Cardini F, Weixin H. Moxibustion for correction of breech presentation: a randomized controlled trial. JAMA 1998;280(18): 1580–1584.
22. Angell M, Kassirer JP. Alternative medicine—the risks of untested and unregulated remedies. N Engl J Med 1998;339(12): 839–841.
23. Defining and describing complementary and alternative medicine. Panel on Definition and Description, CAM Research Methodology Conference, April 1995. Altern Ther Health Med 1997;3(2):49–57.
24. Kaptchuk TJ, Eisenberg DM. Varieties of healing. 2: a taxonomy of unconventional healing practices. AnnIntern Med 2001;135(3):196–204.
25. Zollman C, Vickers A. ABC of complementary medicine: What is complementary medicine? BMJ 1999;319(7211):693–696.
26. Schneiderman, LJ. Alternative medicine or alternatives to medicine? A Physician's Perspective. Camb Q Healthc Ethics 2000;9(1);83–97.
27. Sampson W, Atwood K. Propagation of the absurd: demarcation of the Absurd revisited. Med. J Aust 2005: 183(11–12):580–581.
28. National Center for Complementary and Alternative Medicine. Guidance on Designing Clinical Trials of CAM Therapies: Determining Dose Ranges. http://nccam.nih.gov/research/policies/guideonct.htm. Accessed February 3, 2006.
29. Wear A. Quack. The Lancet 2005;366(9492):1157.
30. Flora K, Hahn M, Rosen H, Benner K. Milk thistle (Silybum marianum) for the therapy of liver disease. Am J Gastroenterol 1998;93(2):139–143.
31. Bell IR, Caspi O, Schwartz GER, et al. Integrative medicine and systemic outcomes research: issues in the emergence of a new

model for primary health care. Arch Intern Med 2002;162(2): 133–140.

32. Gordis L. From Association to Causation: Deriving Inferences from Epidemiologic Studies. In: Gordis L. Epidemiology. Philadelphia, PA: Saunders, 2004, pp. 203–223.

33. Marks HM. The Progress of Experiment: Science and Therapeutic Reform in the United States, 1900–1990. Cambridge, England: Cambridge University Press, 1997.

34. Tunis SR, Stryer DB, Clancy CM. Practical clinical trials: increasing the value of clinical research for decision making in clinical and health policy. JAMA 2003;290(12):1624–1632.

35. Black N. Why we need observational studies to evaluate the effectiveness of health care. BMJ 1996;312(7040):1215–1218.

36. Vickers A. Methodological issues in complementary and alternative medicine research: a personal reflection on 10 years of debate in the United Kingdom. J Altern Complement Med 1996;2(4):515–524.

37. Vickers AJ. Message to complementary and alternative medicine: evidence is a better friend than power. BMC Complement Altern Med 2001;1(1):1.

38. Rothman KJ, Michels KB. The Continuing Unethical Use of Placebo Controls. N Engl J Med 1994;331(6):394–398

39. Hrobjartsson A, Gotzsche PC. Is the placebo powerless? An analysis of clinical trials comparing placebo with no treatment. N Engl J Med 2001;344(21):1594–1602.

40. Benedetti, F, Pollo A, Lopiano L, Lanotte M, Vighetti S, Rainero I. (2003) Conscious expectation and unconscious conditioning in analgesic, motor, and hormonal placebo/nocebo responses, J. Neurosci 2003;23:4315–4323.

41. Miller FG, Rosenstein DL. The nature and power of the placebo effect. J Clin Epidemiol 2006;59:331–335.

42. Brody H. The placebo response—Recent research and implications for family medicine. Journal of Family Practice 2000;49(7):649–654.

43. Walach H. The efficacy paradox in randomized controlled trials of CAM and elsewhere: beware of the placebo trap. J Altern Complement Med 2001;7(3):213–218.

44. Kaptchuk TJ. The placebo effect in alternative medicine: can the performance of a healing ritual have clinical significance? Ann Intern Med 2002;136(11):817–825.
45. Kaptchuk TJ. Effect of interpretive bias on research evidence. BMJ 2003;326(7404):1453–1455.
46. Adams KE, Cohen MH, Eisenberg D, Jonsen AR. Ethical considerations of complementary and alternative medical therapies in conventional medical settings. Ann Intern Med 2002;137(8):660–664.
47. Kligler B, Maizes V, Schachter S, et al. Core competencies in integrative medicine for medical school curricula: a proposal. Acad Med 2004;79(6):521–531.

Index